THE
RAILWAYS
OF
HULL &
EAST
YORKSHIRE

The British
Railways Era

by Michael Thompson

HUTTON PRESS
1992

Published by the Hutton Press Ltd.,
130 Canada Drive, Cherry Burton,
Beverley, East Yorkshire HU17 7SB.

Typeset and Printed by
Image Colourprint Ltd.,
Anlaby, Hull.

ISBN 1 872167 46 2

CONTENTS

DEDICATION

To my brothers Martin and Adrian. And all the staff of
British Railways past and present.

ACKNOWLEDGEMENTS

I would like to express my most grateful thanks to:

My wife Margaret for secretarial duties and support.

All the photographers and societies who have allowed their photographic studies to be used.

Steve Bramley for the timetables.

British Rail Public Relations Department York, for kind permission to use their copyright timetables.

John Morfin for general advice.

The many people who have encouraged and supported this project.

INTRODUCTION

The rural landscape of East Yorkshire is studded with the remains of dismantled railways. The golden age of railway transport having come and gone the track beds are now overgrown with weeds, the cuttings which once echoed to the sound of passing trains have fallen silent, and embankments and other earth works have become the home of wild animals. The once busy station buildings are now private houses or have been levelled for the re-use of the land they occupied.

The process of decline began back in the 1920 - 1930's when the Railway Companies began to reduce the number of train services operating on some branch lines and to close loss making stations.

During the 1939 - 1945 War the railways of the British Isles which were operated under unified management gave sterling service to the war effort. Staff worked long hours and track and rolling stock carried the heavy workload with minimum maintenance.

With the return of peace the big four railway companies the London & North Eastern, the London, Midland & Scottish, the Southern and the Great Western were left with the daunting prospect of finding the capital to replace worn out track work, rolling stock and locomotives. With this in mind the Government decided it was in the nation's best interest to nationalise the railways and on January 1st, 1948 British Railways took over the responsibility of running the railways from the big four private companies.

In the early years there was optimism of a bright new future for the nationalised railways. But during the 1950's the rival road transport increasingly took traffic away from the railways. This, combined with lack of Government funding and bad management, left British Railways announcing large losses.

By the late 1950's the Conservative Government decided that the railway network should be reduced in an attempt to reduce the deficits. This led in March 1963, to the publishing of Dr. Richard Beeching's report on the reshaping of British Railways in which it was suggested that one third of the network should be closed. As the notice of closure of individual lines was posted there was a great outcry from the local public, but this was to be of no avail and closure dates were announced. Then in October 1964, the Conservatives were defeated in the General Election and there were hopes that the new Labour Government would repeal the closure notices and allow the doomed railways to remain open. But this was not the case and, in fact, although it was the Conservative Minister of Transport Ernest Marples who set up the closures, most of the local lines were dismantled whilst Labour Ministers of Transport, Tom Fraser and Barbara Castle were in office.

Although 300,000 railway workers were made redundant due to the restructuring, they did not mount a national campaign. This was possibly due to being unable to obtain support from other major unions in a bid to halt the closures.

The Hull - Bridlington - Scarborough line has survived threat of closure in 1968 and following restructuring of its operation and the granting of subsidies it seems safe for the foreseeable future.

At the present time the passenger service for Hull is served by comfortable modern rolling stock. However the number of through trains continues to decline. The vast amount of rail freight from the Hull Docks has all but disappeared. Most of it travels by motor way on the back of lorries.

RAILWAYS OF HULL AND EAST YORKSHIRE

SEAMER
CAYTON
GRISTHORPE
FILEY
FILEY HOLIDAY CAMP
HUNMANBY
SPEETON
BEMPTON
FLAMBOROUGH
BRIDLINGTON
CARNABY
BURTON AGNES
LOWTHORPE
NAFFERTON
DRIFFIELD

NORTH SEA

MALTON
SETTRINGTON
NORTH GRIMSTON
WHARRAM
BURDALE
SLEDMERE & FIMBER
WETWANG
GARTON

WARTHILL
HOLTBY
EARSWICK
STAMFORD BRIDGE
FANGFOSS
YORK
POCKLINGTON
NUNBURNHOLME
LONDESBOROUGH

SOUTHBURN
HUTTON CRANSWICK
BAINTON
MIDDLETON ON THE WOLDS
LOCKINGTON
ARRAM

HORNSEA TOWN
HORNSEA BRIDGE
WASSAND
SIGGLESTHORNE
WHITEDALE
BURTON CONSTABLE
ELLERBY
SKIRLAUGH
SWINE
SUTTON ON HULL

ENTHORPE
KIPLING COATES
MARKET WEIGHTON
CHERRY BURTON
BEVERLEY
EVERINGHAM

CLIFF COMMON
MENTHORPE GATE
BUBWITH
HIGHFIELD
FOGGATHORPE
HOLME MOOR

HEMINGBROUGH
WRESSLE
NORTH HOWDEN
NORTH EASTRINGTON
SOUTH EASTRINGTON
SANDHOLME
WALLINGFEN
NORTH CAVE
SOUTH CAVE
LITTLE WEIGHTON
COTTINGHAM
SPRINGHEAD HALT

SELBY
DRAX
BARMBY
SOUTH HOWDEN
STADDLETHORPE
WILLERBY & KIRKELLA
MARFLEET
HEDON

CARLTON TOWERS
GOOLE
SALTMARSHE
BROOMFLEET
BROUGH
MELTON HALT
FERRIBY
HESSLE

WITHERNSEA
RYEHILL & BURSTWICK
OTTRINGHAM
KEYINGHAM
WINESTEAD
PATRINGTON

RIVER HUMBER

7

MAP OF HULL DOCKS CIRCA 1952

Under British Transport Commision ownership, there were 10 docks, 12 miles of quays and approximately 300 miles of standard gauge railway traffic.

1. **Botanic Gardens Station**
2. **Stepney Station**
3. **Wilmington Station**
4. **Southcoates Station**
5. **Marfleet Station**
6. **Cannon Street Station**

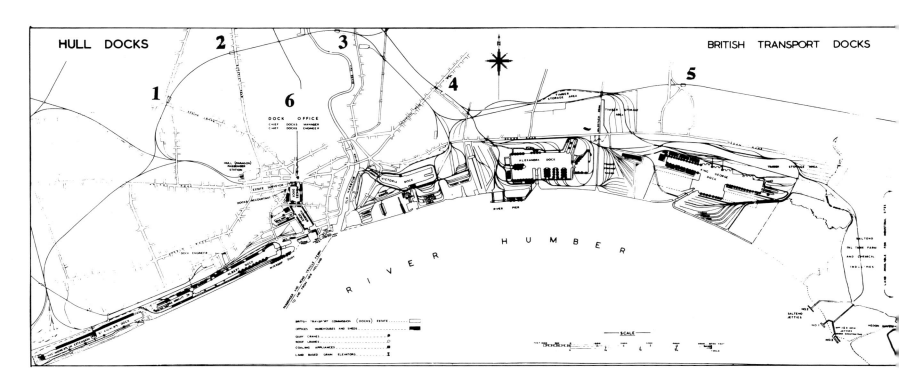

RAILWAYS OF HULL

The growth of the City and Port of Kingston upon Hull, was only made possible by railways. The Hull & Selby, the York & North Midland, the North Eastern, the Hull & Barnsley, the London & North Eastern and British Railways have all played their part.

PASSENGER TRAFFIC

Hull's original passenger station, the Hull & Selby Railway's which was situated at Railway Street and opened in 1840, was soon found to be inadequate and so it was decided to build a new station in Paragon Street which was becoming the new centre of Hull.

The York & North Midland Railway Company entrusted the design of the new station to G.T. Andrews and a tender £51,500 for the construction of the building was accepted on March 1st 1847. Paragon Station was opened on May 8th 1848. The adjoining Royal Station Hotel also designed by G.T. Andrews was opened in 1851.

By the turn of the century the station had become too small to handle the volume of traffic and in 1902, tenders totalling £75,098 were accepted for alterations and additions to the station. This involved rebuilding the original platforms, adding new ones and the construction of a new roof. There were nine full length and one short platforms under cover of the overall roof. And four outdoor platforms situated on the south side, which were intended for excursion traffic. The new station improvements were brought into use on December 12th, 1904.

By the late 1920's there were regular local services to Brough, Beverley, Withernsea and Hornsea. Also Bridlington, Scarborough and York were well served. There were several through long distance services to Kings Cross via Doncaster, Liverpool was served by three routes which gave direct links to Sheffield, Manchester and Leeds. The north to Newcastle was served via York.

In post-war years, the railways have faced increasing competition from road transport. This has resulted in British Railways making drastic cuts in local services. In 1955, the Hull - South Howden service was withdrawn, followed by Hull-Withernsea and Hornsea withdrawn in 1964 and Hull - Market Weighton - York withdrawn in 1965. This has led to the closure of platforms 1-3 and 14. The number of trains using the station over the years was as follows: 1870, 86 trains in and out; 1904, 192; 1931, 268; 1957, 204; 1991, 167.

The front exterior of the station was modernised from 1960, with the building of a new office block, to accommodate the BR Hull Divisional offices which opened in 1962.

DOCKS FREIGHT TRAFFIC

In its heyday, Hull was Britain's third largest commercial and largest deepsea fishing port. The port consisted of eleven docks, with a water area of 200 acres, two riverside quays and three oil jetties. The total length of quays was 12 miles and there were about 300 miles of standard gauge railway line in and around the docks.

In the days when most freight was transported by rail, the traffic to and from Hull's docks was so heavy that trains actually had to queue to get onto the docks. Each dock office reported daily to Hull Wagon Control, to advise them of the situation regarding railway wagons on the dock: the number of empty open wagons, vans and bogie bolsters on hand and how many more were required for loading. Also the number of loaded wagons awaiting dispatch. Train loads of empty wagons were dispatched daily to Hull from Doncaster, Kings Cross, Nottingham, Whitemoor, Woodford and York. Pilot engines took the loaded wagons to the vast marshalling yards west of Hull, where trains were assembled for dispatch to all parts of the British Isles.

At the present time there is a small amount of rail traffic from King George dock and the Saltend refinery.

LOCOMOTIVE SHEDS

During the twentieth century the railways of Hull were served by four locomotive sheds. Dairycoates and Botanic Gardens (North Eastern Railway), Springhead and Alexandra Dock (Hull & Barnsley Railway). Botanic Gardens which is situated near to Paragon Station serviced the passenger locomotive, while Dairycoates which was close to the marshalling yards west of Hull mainly serviced freight locomotives. At one time Dairycoates was the largest shed in the north east of England.

Springhead shed was the headquarters of the Hull & Barnsley

The Alexandra dock shed serviced the dock's shunting engines. At the time of the L.N.E.R. take over in 1923, Dairycoates housed 150 engines, Botanic Gardens 47, Springhead 122 and Alexandra Dock 29. Under British Railways' ownership Dairycoates shed code was 53A 1949-1960, 50B 1960-1967. Its allocations, were: 1950, 145 engines, 1959, 94 engines 1965, 35 engines. Dairycoates closed as a steam shed in June 1967 and completely in 19xx. Botanic Gardens shed code was 53B. Its allocation in 1950 was 50 engines. The shed closed to steam in June 1959, and at the present time it serves as a refuelling depot. Springhead shed code was 50C. Its 1950 allocation was 55 engines. The shed closed in December 1958 but was used for storage for a few more years.

THE HULL & BARNSLEY HIGH LEVEL LINE

The Hull & Barnsley line was carried on an embankment that encircled the city and ran roughly parallel to the North Eastern Railway's Victoria Dock Line. The eastern end of the arc started at Alexandra Dock and was linked to King George Dock, which was jointly owned with The North Eastern Railway. The Western arm terminated at the Neptune Street goods station.

A spur from Sculcoates Junction ran southward to serve the Beverley Road station at Fitzroy Street and the terminus at Cannon Street. Both were closed for passengers in 1924, but Cannon Street remained open for goods until 1964.

VICTORIA DOCK LINE

The Port of Hull's earliest network of four docks:- Queen's Prince's Humber and Railway, were situated in the centre of the town and their freight traffic could be easily handled by the local Railway Street goods station.

With the increasing number of larger vessels arriving at the port the Hull Dock Company found it necessary to build a new dock independent of the Town Dock system. This resulted in the construction of the Victoria Dock, situated to the east of the River Hull and completed in 1850.

The York and North Midland Railway Company, whose marshalling yards lay to the west of the river, realised that it would be necessary to have access to the new dock. In order to achieve this, powers were obtained on June 30th, 1852 to build a railway to serve the dock. The line was 3.25 miles long, branching out of the Hull - Selby line near Anlaby Road, running in a semi-circle round the outskirts of Hull at low level and terminating at the Victoria Dock station, near to Hedon Road.

The line crossed all the main roads leading out of Hull and necessitated the building of six level crossings. Due to the level nature of the land the line was easy to build and opened for freight traffic on May 16th, 1853. The only formidable obstacle was the crossing of the River Hull and this was achieved by construction of a swing bridge. The reason for a swing bridge was that on high tide shipping moved to and from wharves situated up river of the railway. By law shipping has always had the right of way over road and rail traffic.

Once the line was opened a suburban passenger service, (one of the earliest outside of London) began on June 1st, 1853. Trains started from the Railway street station and originally it would seem that passengers were picked up where the railway crossed the main roads. Stations were also built at Stepney, Sculcoates and Southcoates.

At first the service was well patronised but soon interest waned and the number of trains was reduced. Then in October 1854, three months after the York & North Midland Railway became part of the North Eastern Railway, the service ceased altogether. The Victoria Dock line was destined to have no passenger traffic for ten years.

On June 27th, 1854 the Hull and Holderness Railway was opened. For ten years the company's Hull terminus was the Victoria Dock station, which it shared briefly with the York & North Midland. Then in 1864, the Victoria Dock branch was doubled as part of a scheme to allow the Withernsea line trains to run into Paragon station, but due to incomplete signalling the move from Victoria Dock station was delayed until June 1st 1864.

On March 28th, 1864 the Hull & Hornsea Railway was opened. For several weeks trains for Hornsea started from the company's new Wilmington station, then from June 1st, 1864 this service also ran into Paragon Station.

Following the transfer of the Withernsea and Hornsea trains to Paragon Station the Victoria Dock lines suburban stations were gradually reopened and a station was built at Cemetery Gates which in 18xx was renamed Botanic Gardens.
Between 1905 - 1907 the whole layout at Wilmington was re-arranged in order to dispense with a level crossing. This involved the building of a new swing bridge over the River Hull, and later the closure of Sculcoates and the original Wilmington Stations. In their place a new Wilmington station was opened midway between the two in 1912.

Some idea of the importance of the stations on the line in this era can be gathered from the 1911 figures which show that 44,915 passengers used Botanic Gardens, 45,569 used Stepney and 51,275 Southcoates.

During the post-war years the volume of road traffic using the city's main roads rapidly increased and by the late 1950's there was a great deal of agitation from the local bus operators, road haulage companies and car owners, with regard to time lost waiting at Hull's eight main level crossings.

Although the Hull - Hornsea and Hull - Withernsea passenger services were withdrawn in 1964, there was still a large number of dock transfer freight movements. To accommodate this, proposals were drawn up to close the low level line and transfer trains over the high level former Hull & Barnsley line.

On March 21st, 1967 Mrs Barbara Castle the Minister of Transport, agreed to British Railways' proposals for the closure of the Victoria Dock line. In agreeing to the proposals the Minister took into account the fact that the Hull Corporation wished to use the route of the low level line to form an integral part of an intermediate ring road.

The cost of transferring traffic to the high level, removal of track and associated work on the low level, was borne mainly by British Railways. However Hull City Council contributed £150,000 to the project although this included £79,650 granted in August 1967 by the Minister of Transport. With the closure of the Victoria Dock branch in 1968, road traffic in the city centre benefited from the removal six level crossings at Spring Bank, Park Road, Beverley Road, Dansom Lane, Bankside and Holderness Road.

Victoria Dock closed soon after on February 1st 1970. In recent years the dock has been filled in and a housing estate is being built on the site.

A view of Paragon Station looking east circa 1960. The bay to the left was used for goods, the diesel multiple units are on platforms 1 and 2 which were used for Hornsea and Withernsea trains. Tank locomotive No.67686 class V3 2-6-2 is on pilot duties shunting coaches into platform 6, prior to the train engine coming on. The coach on the right is situated on the short number 11 platform.
PHOTOGRAPH D.P. LECKONBY.

View of the north side of Paragon Station on June 6th, 1961 showing the carriage sidings and coal yard. Class B1 4-6-0 No. 61289 runs light to Botanic Gardens motive power depot for servicing before taking its next turn. PHOTOGRAPH ERIC CRACKNELL.

An interior view of Paragon Station. Class V1 2-6-2 tank locomotive No.67640 is waiting to depart with the Hull coaches of the Yorkshire Pullman train, which linked up with the Leeds portion at Doncaster. The complete train then travelled south to London Kings Cross. PHOTOGRAPH NEVILLE STEAD.

13

On March 3rd, 1962 in wintery weather class B16 4-6-0 No.61444 works out of Hull Paragon with an express parcels train, passing the terrace houses of Londesborough Street which backed onto the approach lines to the station.
PHOTOGRAPH BRIAN EGAN.

During the British Railways' steam era, Botanic shed used its allocation of A8, C12, L1,V1 & V3 tank locomotives on Hornsea and Withernsea trains. The train was usually made up of a variety of vintage non-corridor coaches as seen in this mid 1950's scene, with class L1 2-6-4 tank locomotive No. 67763.
PHOTOGRAPH NEVILLE STEAD COLLECTION.

Stepney Station was situated on Beverley Road. This view is looking west towards Park Road level crossing. The six car diesel multiple unit is bound for Withernsea. The station building on the left consisted of the station master's house, waiting rooms and a ticket office. The station master at Stepney also looked after the affairs of the neighbouring Botanic Gardens and Wilmington stations.
PHOTOGRAPH J.F. SEDGWICK.

A heavy freight locomotive Class WD 2-8-0 No.90352 brings a train of empty mineral wagons on past Botanic Gardens shed towards Victoria Crossing on one of the twice daily Wilmington - Hessle Quarry workings.
PHOTOGRAPH DOUG HARDY.

Class A5 4-6-2 tank locomotive No.69802 arriving at Botanic Gardens Station with a train for Withernsea circa 1952. The station was situated at the junction of Princes Avenue and Springbank. The photograph illustrates the valuable role station staff played in chatting with passengers and assisting them with heavy items.
PHOTOGRAPH AUTHOR'S COLLECTION.

16

Wilmington Station was situated between Bankside and Cleveland Street, a busy industrial area of the city. This was the second Wilmington station and was opened in 1912 following the rearrangement of the Victoria Dock line in the area. The station was at a raised level with the booking office and waiting room down in Foster Street. PHOTOGRAPH J.F. SEDGWICK.

Wilmington Bridge carried the Victoria Dock line over the River Hull. The present bridge was opened in 1912 and replaced the original swing bridge which was only single track. Although the railway line is disused the bridge has been retained as a public right of way. It is still manned at tide time to allow shipping to pass through. PHOTOGRAPH D.P. LECKONBY.

View of the Victoria Dock line looking east towards Dansom Lane. The train to the left is coming off the Hornsea branch. To the right is the Wilmington goods yard and office. In the foreground is the bridge carrying the line over Cleveland Street. PHOTOGRAPH MICHAEL CLARKE.

A Permanent Way gang at work getting a derailed mineral train back on the track at Wilmington with the assistance of Dairycoates steam crane, during the late 1960's. PHOTOGRAPH MICHAEL CLARKE.

Approaching Southcoates station, an eight car diesel multiple unit on the Hull - Withernsea service passes through Southcoates level crossing on Holderness Road.
PHOTOGRAPH D.P. LECKONBY.

Class WD 2-8-0 No.90482 comes off Alexandra Dock onto the High level line on a trip working in September 1964. Alexandra Dock closed to commercial shipping on September 30th, 1982. The track was removed and bridges dismantled in January 1988. PHOTOGRAPH DOUG HARDY.

Class A7 tank locomotive No.69783 with a train of empty coal wagons heads west past Sculcoates Junction. The lines to the right lead to Cannon Street. The building is the disused former Hull & Barnsley Railway Beverley Road Station. In the background is Sculcoates Power Station which was opened in 1895 on a site bounded by the Hull & Barnsley Railway which transported the coal for fuel, and the Barmston drain which supplied the cooling water. PHOTOGRAPH J. OXLEY.

An English Electric Type 4 (class 40) diesel electric locomotive No.346 heads a fully fitted freight over Springbank West. The signals indicate that the train is taking the spur down to the low level Hull - Bridlington line at Walton Street to gain access to the main line out of Hull on September 6th, 1966. PHOTOGRAPH ERIC CRACKNELL.

Whilst working a train of empty stock from Springhead, class J39/1 0-6-0 No.64831 halts at Springbank South signalbox for the delivery of a churn of fresh water for the signalmen. A large number of signalboxes and gatehouses throughout the railway network relied on trains to deliver their supply of drinking water and supplies. PHOTOGRAPH NEVILLE STEAD.

Ivat Class 4 MT 2-6-0 No.43079 heads for Paragon Station past Springbank South signalbox from the Boothferry Park halt which was opened for football supporters trains in 1951. With a Hull City v Workington Town football special on Saturday August 29th, 1964. The match result was a 2-2 draw. PHOTOGRAPH DOUG HARDY.

A view of the former Hull & Barnsley Railway's Neptune Street Goods Station with Class WD 2-8-0 No.90571 about to leave the yard with a pick up goods for all stations on the former Hull & Barnsley up to Carlton. This service was withdrawn from April 1959. PHOTOGRAPH NEVILLE STEAD.

Engine class B1 4-6-0 No.61012 "Puku" brings a train of fitted vans down off the high level at Hessle Road in February 1964, following the building of the "flyover" which resulted in the line being rearranged to join the Hull - Selby at low level and pass under the road bridge.
PHOTOGRAPH BRIAN EGAN.

Neptune Street Goods Yard in March 1968. Burners are cutting up Stanier class 8F 2-8-0 No. 48214. Albert Draper & Son the Hull scrap metal merchant leased the former Hull & Barnsley Railway goods yards at Sculcoates and Neptune street for breaking up redundant rolling stock. Between 1963 - 1969, 732 locomotives were scrapped at these yards. Neptune street yard closed in 1984. PHOTOGRAPH MICHAEL CLARKE.

English Electric Type 5 (class 55 "Deltic") locomotive No.55019 "Royal Highland Fusilier" crossing over the dismantled Newington branch on the former Hull & Barnsley line with an afternoon Kings Cross - Hull train on October 7th, 1979. Trains had been diverted via the high level line because of engineering work between Hessle Road and West Parade. PHOTOGRAPH M.R. LAKE.

Dairycoates shed class K3 2-6-0 No.61819 heads north to Bridlington with an excursion across Newington level crossing on Anlaby Road. The Newington branch was the section of track between Hessle Road Junction and Cottingham South Junction. It was originally part of the Bridlington branch which became redundant on the opening of Paragon Station. The line was used for trains working through Hull but not calling at Paragon Station. The Newington branch closed on September 13th, 1965.
PHOTOGRAPH D.P. LECKONBY.

British Railways standard class 3 2-6-0 No. 77012 heads south past Waterworks Crossing with an inspector's coach in the early 1960's.
PHOTOGRAPH A.E. SLOAN

On the quayside at King George Dock circa 1952, lines of insulated railway vans are ready to be loaded with cargo from the Shaw, Saville & Albion line vessel **Athenic**. Having arrived from Australia the cargo would consist of chilled meat, fruit and wool.
PHOTOGRAPH INNES STUDIO - HESSLE.

Two class J72 O-6-O tank engines Nos.69009-69010 (part of the class which were built by British Railways) on shunting duties at Alexandra Dock on July 9th, 1960. These engines worked the vans and wagons to and from the dock sidings to the quays where porters and loaders handled the ships' cargoes.
PHOTOGRAPH D. LOVEDAY (GRESLEY SOCIETY).

An aerial view of the Town Docks circa 1954, with the Central Goods Depot on the lower left. In the adjoining Humber Dock are two railway ships (Associated Humber Lines) which were engaged on the near continental trade.
PHOTOGRAPH INNES STUDIO - HESSLE.

Class J72 0-6-0 tank engine No.69009 on shunting duties on the south side of Albert Dock/Riverside Quay sidings. This area was badly damaged during the 1939-1945 War and was rebuilt during the 1950's. PHOTOGRAPH IAN SCOTNEY.

A class J77 0-6-0 tank engine No.68409 brings a train of empty fish vans onto the North side of St. Andrew's Dock to the fish quays in 1955. The vans would form the various fish trains that would leave the dock later in the day. In their heyday Hull's 8 fish trains served 1,000 stations and 4,000 distribution points. PHOTOGRAPH NEVILLE STEAD.

Class J25 O-6-O No.65693 heads towards Hessle Road from Dairycoates with a trip working to the eastern docks. PHOTOGRAPH NEVILLE STEAD.

On January 20th, 1967 near to the end of steam engine working in the Hull area Class WD 2-8-O No.90378 heads west down the Manor House branch with a freight train past Dairycoates shed, with two English Electric type 3 diesel electric locomotives in the background. PHOTOGRAPH BRIAN EGAN.

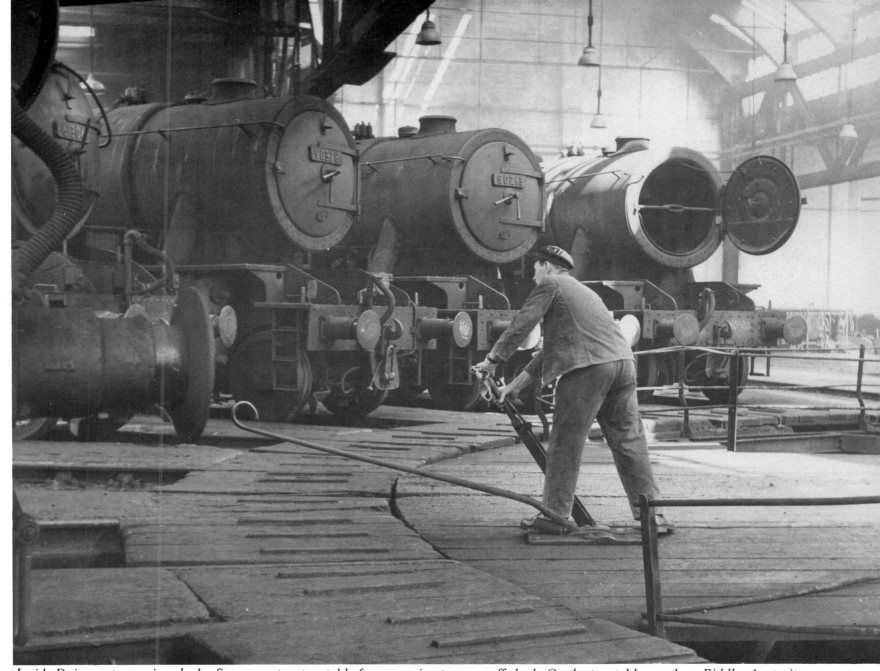

Inside Dairycoates engine shed a fireman sets a turntable for an engine to come off shed. On the turntable are three Riddles Austerity ex-War Department engines, one of the main classes of 2-8-O freight engines to operate in the Hull area in the post-war years. The other engine is a Thompson class B1 4-6-O No.61306. Dairycoates was the largest shed in the north eastern region. The roundhouse was equipped with 6 turntables. Coded 53A in 1949, the shed was recoded 50B in 1960.
The last of the steam engine allocation departed in June 1967.
PHOTOGRAPH AUTHOR'S COLLECTION.

Springhead wagon repair staff circa 1950.
PHOTOGRAPH L. DRIFFILL.

Botanic Garden shed (coded 53B) is situated to the west of Paragon Station and mainly handled the area's passenger locomotives. This view in the mid 1950's shows Class B1 4-6-0 No.61248 "Geoffrey Gibbs", D49/2 4-4-0 No.62754 "The Berkeley", A8 4-6-2 No.69894 and L1 2-6-4 No.67763. The shed lost its steam engine allocation in June 1959 despite a major rebuild two years earlier. The majority of the stock went to neighbouring Dairycoates. Botanic shed continued to service locomotives until the late 1980's. At the present time it serves as a refuelling depot. PHOTOGRAPH A.J. WICKENS.

A view of the Springhead shed (coded 53C) and locomotive works in the late 1950's, with Class WD No.90571 shunting freight in the yard. In the background the former 8 road engine shed is in a state of disrepair and used for storing diesel multiple units. Although the shed lost its allocation in December 1959 when the last engines were transferred to Dairycoates, Springhead was still used for storing engines for a few more years. PHOTOGRAPH NEVILLE STEAD.

Alexandra Dock shed (stabling point) was situated at the north east corner of the dock close to the graving (dry) docks. At weekends the shed's allocation of J72 shunting engines lay idle. Following the closure of the shed the engines were linked together and returned to Dairycoates shed at weekends.
PHOTOGRAPH NEVILLE STEAD COLLECTION.

VICTORIA DOCK BRANCH

CANNON STREET TO SPRINGHEAD

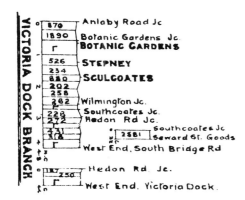

CANNON STREET

Bridge over N.E.R.

Beverley road Jnc.

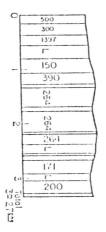

NEPTUNE STREET GOODS

Outward Sidings

Liverpool Street Jnc.

Junc. with N.E.R.

Springbank South Jnc.

Springbank West Jnc.

Springhead Sidings

Locomotive Jnc.

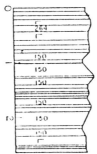

ALEXANDRA DOCK

Alexandra Dock Jnc.

Bridges Jnc.

Burleigh Street Siding

River Hull Swing Bridge

Sculcoates Goods Jnc.

Beverley road Jnc.

Beverley Road Jnc.

Ella Street

Springbank North Jnc.

SPRINGHEAD LOCO. SHED

THE HULL & SELBY RAILWAY

With the building of the Leeds - Selby Railway between 1830 and 1834 there was great disappointment with certain business interests in Hull that the line was not be be extended through to the Humber port. The advantages of a railway linking Hull to Leeds and Manchester were most apparent.

John Exley, a Hull customs officer, took a leading role in directing public attention to the necessity of the line and articles supporting the project were featured in the Hull newspapers of the time.

The Hull bankers George Liddell and James Henwood were among those who took the initiative to raise the £20,000 needed to satisfy the requirements of the Parliamentary standing order for the railway bill to be sponsored.

Following a survey of the line a prospectus was issued to subscribers for a Hull - Selby Railway on July 26th, 1834. With the raising of the necessary capital and the appeasement of several landowners to the west of Hull, the Hull & Selby Railway Company Act of Parliament Bill received Royal Assent on June 21st, 1836.

The original intention was to have stations at Welton and at North and South Cave, but due to opposition to the railway by the Raikes family of Welton a more southerly route with a station at Brough was chosen.

Although the line was built on level ground, it took four years to complete the 30.75 miles of track. To gain access to Selby station a swing bridge had to be built over the River Ouse. The Hull & Selby Railway was opened on July 1st, 1840. The company's Hull terminus was situated to the west of Humber Dock, with its principal entrance in Railway Street.

From July 1st, 1845 the Hull & Selby Railway Company was leased to the York & North Midland Railway Company. However it retained a separate identity and name until incorporated into the North Eastern Railway in 1872.

On July 22nd, 1847 an act was passed authorising a new passenger station in Paragon Street near to the city centre. Three new sections of line linked the new station to the Hull - Selby and Hull - Scarborough lines.

With the opening of Paragon Station on May 8th, 1848 the Railway Street station was closed to regular passenger traffic and became Hull's main goods depot. Later it became known as the Manor House Street Station, and the section of track to Dairycoates the Manor House Branch.

HULL - DONCASTER LINE

The opening of the line between Thorne - Goole - Staddlethorpe on July 30th, 1869, by the North Eastern Railway Company created a new through route for Hull - Doncaster trains. Prior to the opening of the new line train workings for the south were routed via Milford Junction.

By the turn of the century due to the increased volume of traffic using the railway, it became necessary to upgrade the section of line between Hessle East and Staddlethorpe to four tracks. When the work of widening the track took place in 1904, it involved many alterations to the buildings and layout of the stations. Hessle, Ferriby, Broomfleet and Staddlethorpe acquired platforms on the outer slow lines, but Brough had platforms on all four lines. As the major part of the widening took place on the south side of the track this allowed some of the earlier buildings to be retained on the down (north) side.

The main Hull freight yards were situated between Dairycoates and Hessle. The Inward and Mineral yards which were developed in 1909 and the Priory extension were on the down (north) side of the main line. The outward yard was on the up line.

In 1907, authority was given for a rearrangement of the track entering Hull from the west. This involved the construction of a 179 foot span girder bridge over the lines connecting the yards to the north and south of the passenger line.

In 1920, Melton Halt was opened for the use of employees of the local Earles Cement works. Also dating from the 1920's is the service to Brough for the Blackburn Aircraft workers.

As the population and size of Hull increased, many of the more affluent families moved out into the suburbs. Eventually a suburban service was warranted and so on April 8th, 1929 the London & North Eastern Railway introduced a regular half hourly service between Hull, Hessle, Ferriby and Brough.

In December 1935, the new Inward Yard was opened. This yard was equipped with hump, wagon retarders, floodlights and a control tower. Each of the 6 reception roads could hold 100 wagons and the 30 sidings offered a total capacity for 3,000 wagons.

During the early British Railways' years the line was heavily used. In the mid 1950's there were an average of 122 passenger and over 80 freight workings per day. Signal boxes were constantly manned, with signalmen working three eight-hour shifts.

Only two passenger stations were recommended for closure in the Beeching report. These were Hemingbrough which was closed in 1967 and Wressle which remains open. On February 1st, 1974 Staddlethorpe was renamed Gilberdyke.

Following the implementation of the "Beeching report" there was a drastic reduction in the amount of rail freight from the docks, in favour of road haulage. In July 1964, the number of fish trains was reduced from eight to two a day. Finally in 1965 the service which had been reduced to one train a day to London closed altogether. The loss of freight traffic has led to the gradual closure of Hull's network of goods yards. The last of the original pre-war goods yards the, "new inward yard," closed in March 1984. This coincided with the opening of a new yard linked to the main line.

In recent years, there have been several cost cutting operations, including the removal of sections of track and some signal boxes. From 1989 all but Brough station have become unstaffed. The line between Hull - Gilberdyke has reverted back to double track, with the exception of a section between Ferriby and the Melton Cement works sidings which still has 3 tracks.

The recent withdrawl of the nightshift, with the closure of the line's signal boxes between 23.20 to 0510, has occasionally led to the passengers of late running trains to Hull having to be taken to their destination by road transport from York, Selby and Doncaster.

Class A3 4-6-2 "Columbo" waiting to depart with the 4.30pm Hull - Liverpool (Lime Street) train on July 30th, 1960. This service provided some top class engines much to the delight of the young train spotters as seen on the platform.
PHOTOGRAPH M.R. LAKE.

One of the versatile class K3 2-6-O engines No.61875 at Anlaby Road level crossing on the "Yorkshire Pullman" circa 1957. The crossing was replaced by a flyover in April 1965.
PHOTOGRAPH C.T. GOODE.

Heading east along Selby Street towards Paragon Station class D20 4-4-O No.62386 is piloting class B1 4-6-O No.61035 "Pronghorn" on a Leeds - Hull train.
PHOTOGRAPH NEVILLE STEAD COLLECTION.

One of the new "Trans-Pennine" diesel railcar trains approaching Hessle Road level crossing in 1961, on the Hull - Leeds - Manchester Victoria - Liverpool Lime Street service. These trains gave sterling service and remained operational until the mid 1980's.
PHOTOGRAPH NEVILLE STEAD COLLECTION.

Class D49 4-4-O "The Quorn" turns west out of Hull past the Hessle Road signalbox with a train to Leeds. The two bridges were part of the former Hull and Barnsley high level branch line, which were dismantled when the line was brought down to join the former North Eastern line prior to the building of Hessle Road flyover which opened in 1962.
PHOTOGRAPH NEVILLE STEAD.

An express passenger train heads west out of Hull past Hessle East signalbox. The engine class B1 4-6-O No.61306 has been preserved and named "Mayflower". The class of 410 engines were nicknamed "Bongo's", as the first 40 of the class were named after South African antelopes.
PHOTOGRAPH NEVILLE STEAD COLLECTION.

The interior of Hessle Haven signalbox in 1961. The layout is of typical North Eastern Railway design.
PHOTOGRAPH NEVILLE STEAD COLLECTION.

A class G5 O-4-4 tank engine No.67273 fitted for push and pull working calls at Hessle station whilst working a Hull - Hessle - Ferriby - Brough suburban passenger service on September 7th 1954.
PHOTOGRAPH NEVILLE STEAD COLLECTION.

The view of Hessle station looking east on June 23rd, 1966 showing the 4 line track layout. An unidentified class WD 2-8-O is leaving the station siding with a cement train onto the up slow line. The recently built Clive Sullivan Way trunk road runs close to the south of the station through where the coal yard was situated.
PHOTOGRAPH DOUG HARDY.

43

Working trip No.J32 to Hull mineral yard class WD engine No.90482 comes through Ferriby with a train made up of old wooden and modern steel hoppers on August 29th, 1962. Freight trains were normally run on the middle fast lines leaving the slow lines clear for passenger trains to call at the platforms. PHOTOGRAPH M.R. LAKE.

Passing through Melton Halt on the up fast line is class K3 2-6-O engine No.61846 with a fish train. Fish, fruit, meat and perishable goods were transported in special insulated vans and were worked by top link express mixed traffic engines. These trains even had priority over certain passenger trains. PHOTOGRAPH NEVILLE STEAD.

A view of Brough station looking east towards Hull. The outer platforms were used by the suburban services and the inner ones for the main line services. The fine pagoda waiting rooms were recently demolished and replaced by modern shelters.
PHOTOGRAPH DOUGLAS THOMPSON.

At Crabley Creek farm crossing signalman Michael Clarke supervises a herd of cattle across the busy main line. The reason this signalbox has survived the modernisation program is that the line divides the land of the local farm, so in the interests of safety the box is manned during the hours of train services.
PHOTOGRAPH MICHAEL CLARKE.

Class B1 4-6-O No.61080 passes Brough West signalbox with the Hull section of the 10-30 am Kings Cross - Leeds train. At Doncaster the train was split into two sections. One carried on to Leeds and the other to Hull.
PHOTOGRAPH ERIC CRACKNELL.

A view of Broomfleet station looking east. Originally this rural station was only open on market days until 1907, then as required until 1920 when a full service was initiated. PHOTOGRAPH DOUGLAS THOMPSON.

Brush type 4 diesel electric locomotive No.47 102 passes through Gilberdyke (formerly Staddlethorpe) with the 18.50 pm Hull - Leeds Freightliner in June 1984.
PHOTOGRAPH MIKE THOMPSON.

British Railways standard class 5 engine No.73141, heading home with an excursion from the coast on August 8th 1967, thunders through the former North Eastern Railway station at Howden which was renamed from North Howden on June 12th, 1961.
PHOTOGRAPH DOUG HARDY.

Leeds Neville Hill shed class B1 4-6-O No.61237 heads east through Hemingbrough station with a Leeds to Hull train. Although it served a larger community than several others on the Hull - Selby line, Hemingbrough is the only station to have been closed. Recommended for closure in the Beeching report the service was withdrawn on November 6th, 1967.
PHOTOGRAPH H.B. PRIESTLEY (NEVILLE STEAD COLLECTION).

March shed class V2 2-6-2 engine No.60948 comes off the Selby swing bridge over the River Ouse into Selby station with a passenger train working. Once a very busy station serving the east coast main line as well as the cross country routes, Selby is a lot quieter these days.
PHOTOGRAPH J.F. SEDGWICK.

The main feature of the Staddlethorpe (Gilberdyke) Jnc - Goole line is the swing bridge over the River Ouse near to the Port of Goole. The bridge which is 830 feet in length spans the shipping channel and has often been damaged by ships. On December 21st 1973 a German coaster caused considerable damage to the bridge which put the line out of action until August 1974. Shipping has the right of way at the swing bridge and at high tide trains have to wait for ships to pass through. PHOTOGRAPH J.W. ARMSTRONG.

A train for the Goole - Selby branch line service stands at Goole station, with class G5 4-4-O tank locomotive No.67250 in the early 1950's. The last engines of this class were withdrawn in 1958, when their duties were taken over by diesel railcars. PHOTOGRAPH LANCE BROWN (NEVILLE STEAD COLLECTION).

50

SELBY TO DRIFFIELD

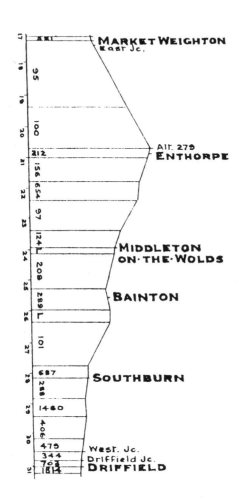

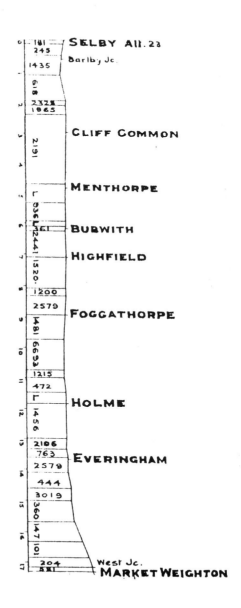

51

Table 24

HULL, SELBY and LEEDS

WEEKDAYS

Miles				am	am	am	am	am	am	J 11 25	SO 10a52	K 12 3	pm	pm 12c15	R 12 50	pm	pm 12 24	SO 2 12	pm	pm 1h55
	25 Bridlington	dep		....	....	....	6n25	8 0	9 12			12 3					2 2		2 50	4 2
—	HULL	dep		5 30	..	7 0	7 50	9 2	10 42			12 3	12 22	1 10			2 2		2 50	4 2
4½	Hessle	"	B	5 40	..	8 0							12 32						3 0	
7½	Ferriby	"		5 46	..	8 6							12 38						3 6	
10½	Brough	"		5 55	..	7 18	8 12	9 18				12 20	12 44						3 12	
14½	Broomfleet	"	C		..								12 51							
17	Staddlethorpe	"		6F 6	..		8 23					12 31	12 57						3 23	
19½	South Eastrington	"			..	7 31	8 29						1 3						3 29	
22½	North Howden	"		6 18	..	7 37	8 35					12 38	1 9						3 35	
25	Wressle	"			..		8 40						1 14						3 40	
28	Hemingbrough	"		6 27	..	7 48	8 46						1 20						3 46	
30½	Selby	arr		6 33	..	7 54	8 54	9 42	11 18			12 51	1 26	1 46				2 38		3 53	4 38
44½	1 York	arr		7 13	..	8 26	..	..	11 58								3 51		5 19	5 19
—	Selby	dep		6 35	7 22	7 56	7 56	9 45	11 20			12 53		1 49			2 12	2 40	3 57	4 40
35½	Hambleton	"			7 30	8 4	9 4											2 21			
—	Sheffield (Mid.)	arr		8E54	10Et33	10Eu48	11E13	11E55	1E26			3E31		3E40			4Ev50		6E32	6E32
38½	South Milford	dep		6 48	7 38	8 12	9 12			12 47	1 10		2 29						4 9	
42	Micklefield	"		6 55	7 45	8 19	9 19		11 33	12 54	1 17	1 28	2 33						4 16	
44½	Garforth	"		7 1	7 51	8 25			11 40	1 1	1 23	1 34	2 44						4 22	
47½	Cross Gates	"	A	7 7	7 57	8 31	9 28		11 49	1 8	1 29	1 40	2 50						4 28	
49	Osmondthorpe	"		7 11	8 1	8 35					1 33		2 54						4 32	
51	LEEDS { Marsh Lane	"		7 16	8 6	8 40					1 38		2 59							
51½	{ City	arr		7 19	8 9	8 43	9 37	10 12	11 58	1 17	1 41	1 49	3 2	2 18	2d30	3 2	3 12	3 55	4 38	5 7
62	9 Bradford (Exchange)	arr		8 12	8 56	10y 4	10x51	11q35	1 0		3 0	3 0		3 51		3 51	3 51	5 7	5b23	5P54
65½	" (Forster Sq.)			8 44		9 55		11 4	12 57								5 4	5 4		6 25
79	Huddersfield			8 14	8 58	9 44	10M30	10 49	1Q24	2 9		2m34	3x37	3 40		3 54	5 4	5 27	5 44
94½	Manchester (Exchange)			9 3	10 5	10 39	11V26	11 38	2e15			3m22	4S18	4 18		4 47	6 27		6 42
126½	Liverpool (Lime St)			10N23	11 6			12k32	3 8			5f 4				5 50	7N34		7 41
182½	Llandudno			12D15	1j28	1g54		3 5	6L45			5mS6	7S13	7 3		8w 3			10 53
94½	Stockport			9 20	9 56			12 1	2G13							5 13			7 10
119½	Crewe			10 16	10 57	12U20		12 45	3 55			5W17		6 18					7 58
153½	Shrewsbury			10H47				2r10	4 55			6W19							8 30
203	Hereford			12H34				3r36	6 14			8 11							9 10
246½	Newport			2H 3				5 7	7 35			10 36							10 32
258½	Cardiff (Gen.)			2H26				5 33	7 55			11 0							12 0
267½	Swansea (Vic.)			4Z17				6 58	9 44			12*45							12 35
																				4* 7

Vertical column notes:
- Refreshment Car—Hull to Liverpool (Lime St.)
- Through Train—Hull to Bradford (Forster Square)
- Through Train—Bridlington to Leeds via Enthorpe
- (dep 11.37 am) and Bridlington to Leeds
- Through Train—Filey Holiday Camp (dep 11.37 am) to Manchester (Exchange)
- Through Train—Filey Holiday Camp (dep. 12.22 pm) to Manchester (Exchange)
- Through Train—Hull to Liverpool (Lime St.)
- Through Train—Bridlington to Leeds via Enthorpe
- Refreshment Car—Hull to Liverpool (Lime St.)

A—For complete service between Micklefield and Leeds see Table 32.
B—For complete service between Hull and Brough see Table 21.
C—For other trains between Brough and Staddlethorpe see Table 16.
D—Saturdays only. Not after 12th September.
E—Via Leeds (City).
F—Calls on Monday only to take up.
G—Until 18th June and from 20th June to 25th June, also on 27th June, arrives Stockport 2.45 pm.
H—On Saturdays arrives Shrewsbury 11.12 a.m. Hereford 12.27 pm, Newport 2.9 pm and Cardiff (Gen.) 2.30 pm.
J—Saturdays only. Runs 4th July to 12th September inclusive.
K—Saturdays only. Commences 4th July.
L—On Saturdays arrives Llandudno 5.49 pm.

M—Applies Saturdays only until 12th September. From 4th July to 5th September inclusive, arrives Huddersfield 10.19 am.
N—Liverpool (Ex)—Passengers change from Exchange to Victoria Station at Manchester.
P—On Saturdays arrives Bradford (Ex) 6.15 pm.
Q—On Fridays 19th and 26th June and Saturdays excepted commencing 29th June arrives Huddersfield 1.5 pm and on Saturdays arrives Huddersfield 12.48 pm.
R—Saturdays only.
S or SO—Saturdays only.
U—Via Manchester (Exchange) and (London Rd.).
V—Applies Saturdays only until 12th September inclusive.
W—Via Manchester (Ex.) and (London Rd.) and applies until 29th August inclusive.
Z—On Saturdays 18th July to 29th August inclusive arrives 4.6 pm. On other Saturdays arrives 4.51 pm. Passengers can arrive Swansea

Passengers changing stations at Manchester do so at their own expense.

(High Street) 3.49 pm. SX (3.53 pm. SO) via Cardiff.
a—am.
b—On Saturdays arrives Bradford (Exchange) 5.42 pm.
c—On Saturdays and Leeds to set down on 13th, 20th and 27th June only.
d—Calls at Selby and Leeds to set down on 13th, 20th and 27th June only.
e—On Fridays 19th and 26th June and daily commencing 29th June arrives Manchester (Ex.) 2.3 pm.
f—Liverpool (Ex.) via Manchester (Ex.) and (Vic.) and applies until 29th August inclusive.
g—Saturdays only. Runs 4th July to 12th September. On 19th September arrives 2.25 pm. On 19th September arrives 3.5 pm.
h—On Saturdays 4th July to 29th August inclusive leaves Bridlington 2.50 pm.
j—Until 26th June and commencing 14th Sept., also Tuesdays, Wednesdays and Thursdays 1st

to 10th Sept. arrives Llandudno 2.10 pm. On Saturdays arrives 1.5 pm.
k—On Sats arrives Liverpool (Lime St) 12.34 pm.
m—Applies until 29th August inclusive.
n—Passengers for beyond Selby leave Bridlington 7.0 am via Enthorpe.
q—On Saturdays arrives Bradford (Ex) 11.32 am.
r—On Saturdays arrives Shrewsbury 2.0 pm Hereford 3.28 pm.
t—On Saturdays arrives Sheffield (Midland) 9E46 am.
u—On Saturdays arrives Sheffield (Midland) 10E45 am.
v—On Fridays and Saturdays arrives Sheffield (Midland) 4E30 pm.
w—On Saturdays arrives Llandudno 8.32 pm.
x—On Saturdays arrives Huddersfield 3.16 pm.
y—On Saturdays arrives 10.9 am.
z—On Saturdays arrives 10.55 am.
*—Swansea (High Street) via Cardiff.

Table 24—continued   HULL, SELBY and LEEDS

		WEEKDAYS—continued							SUNDAYS							
		pm 3F31	pm	pm 5 23	pm 7 48 (L)	pm 7 14			am	am	pm 11a17	pm 1 35	pm	pm	pm 7 50	pm
25 Bridlington	dep	3F31	....	5 23	7 48	7 14					11a17	1 35			7 50	
HULL	dep	5 0	5 15	7 10	..	8 35			7 0	8 40	1 45	3 25	6 40	7 0	..	8 40
Hessle	,,	....	5 25						7 10					7 10		
Ferriby	,,		5 31	...					7 16					7 16		
Brough	,,	5 17	5 39	7 27					7 25			3 42		7 22		
Broomfleet	,,		5 47													
Staddlethorpe	,,		5 51						7 36					7 33		
South Eastrington	,,		5 57	7 39					7 42					7 39		
North Howden	,,	5 31	6 3	7 45					7 48					7 45		
Wressle	,,		6 8	7 50					7 53					7 50		
Hemingbrough	,,		6 16	7 56					7 59					7 56		
Selby	arr	5 43	6 22	8 2	8 53	9 19			8 5	9 16	2 21	4 6	7 16	8 2	8 55	9 21
1 York	arr	6 14	FSO	FSX 8 47		12c32				10 8		5 15	7Q50	8 35		10 1
Selby	dep	5 45	6 25	6 33	8 4	8 54	9 25	9 32	8 8	9 18	2 26	4 9	7 20	8 5	8 56	9 27 9 32
Hambleton		5 53														
Sheffield (Mid.)	arr		8Y15		10Ex42	11E 8	10d49		11E 2	11E14	5E 7	6Y20	9Y31	11E 8	11E 8	10d57
South Milford	dep	6 1	6 42	6 50	8 16	9 8	9 46		8 22			4 26		8 17	9W10	9 44
Micklefield			6 49	6 57		9 14	9 55		8 29					8 24	9W17	9 51
Garforth		6 12	6 55	7 3		9 20	10 1		8 35		2 46			8 30	9W23	9 57
Cross Gates		6 18	7 1	7 9		9 26	10 7		8 41		2 52			8 36	9W29	10 3
Osmondthorpe		6 22	7 5	7 13												
LEEDS Marsh Lane			7 10	7 18												
City	arr	6 28	7 18	7 24	8 35	9 36	10 16		8 50	9 45	3 0	4 42		8 45	9 38	10 12
9 Bradford (Exchange)	arr	7 45	9 5	9 5	9 31	10 46	11 25			10 43	4 23	5 24		9 58	10 49	11 5
(Forster Sq.)	,,	7J 0	8t16		10 33	11 37				11 8	5 24	6 35				10 57
Huddersfield	,,	7M47	8 56	8 56	10V22	10R59	11 11			12K32	6b46	7 34				12a34
Manchester (Exchange)	,,	8M41	10 22	10 22		12a34				12K32	3 10	10 13				12a34
Liverpool (Lime St.)	,,	9M37	11T52	11 52		2r58				7 3		10 59				2 58
Llandudno	,,					4X54										4x54
Stockport	,,		9 47		12D 5	12 18				7 2						12 18
Crewe	,,		10 46		12D50	1 11				2U58	7 56	11U29				1 11
Shrewsbury	,,		11h15	1n 0	2D10	2 10				5U 2	10 51					2 10
Hereford	,,		12h32	2m17	4 7	4k 7				6 53						4 7
Newport	,,				4 45					8 32						4 45
Cardiff (Gen.)	,,				5 12					8 55						5 12
Swansea (Vic.)	,,				8y 4	11* 0										8w 4

Vertical column labels (Weekdays): "Through Train—Bridlington to Leeds via Enthorpe"; "Pontefract (arr 9.50 pm)". *Vertical column labels (Sundays):* "Through Train—Hull to York"; "Through Train—Bridlington to Leeds via Enthorpe"; "Pontefract (arr 9.53 pm)".

A—For complete service between Micklefield and Leeds see Table 32.
B—For complete service between Hull and Brough see Table 21.
C—For other trains between Brough and Staddlethorpe see Table 16.
D—Applies Saturday mornings only 4th July to 22nd August inclusive.
E—*Via* Leeds (City).
F—From 29th June to 29th August inclusive passengers for beyond Selby depart Bridlington 3.45 pm, *via* Enthorpe.
FSO—Fridays and Saturdays only.
FSX—Fridays and Saturdays excepted.

J—On Saturdays arrives 7.5 pm.
K—Calls at Manchester (Victoria) 3 minutes earlier.
L—Runs 29th June to 12th September inclusive.
M—On Fridays arrives Huddersfield 7.21, Manchester (Vic.) 8.13, Liverpool (Ex.) 9.15 pm.
Q—*Via* Church Fenton.
R—On Saturdays arrives Huddersfield 10.39 pm.
T—On Saturdays arrives Liverpool (Lime St.) 11.58 pm.
U—*Via* Manchester (Exchange) and (London Road).
V—On Saturdays arrives Huddersfield 9.58 pm.

W—Sets down only.
X—*Via* Crewe. Sunday mornings excepted.
Y—Sheffield (Victoria) connection at Selby and Doncaster.
a—am.
b—Calls at Manchester (Victoria) 6.44 pm.
c—Sunday mornings excepted.
d—Connection at Pontefract.
h—*Via* Manchester (Exchange) and (London Rd.). Applies on Fridays only 3rd July to 28th August.
k—On Sunday mornings arrives 3.55 am.
m—Saturday mornings and not after 12th September. On 19th September arrives 2.53 pm.

n—Friday nights only and note " U " applies.
r—am. On Sunday mornings arrives 3.8 am.
t—Saturdays only.
w—Passengers can arrive Swansea (High St.) 7.25 am *via* Cardiff.
x—On Fridays arrives Sheffield 10E23 pm.
y—Sunday mornings excepted. Passengers can arrive Swansea (High St.) 7.25 am (7.50 am on Sundays) *via* Cardiff.
z—*Via* Crewe.
*—Swansea (High Street) *via* Cardiff.

Passengers changing stations at Manchester do so at their own expense.

HULL - BRIDLINGTON - SCARBOROUGH

Following the opening of the Hull and Selby Railway in 1840, which secured the through connection between Hull and Leeds, the Company drew up plans for a railway between Hull and Bridlington. This was to deter any schemes by locally interested parties attempting to connect West Yorkshire and Bridlington.

The Hull & Selby Railway Company obtained the necessary Act of Parliament to build the line in 1845.

At about the same time George Hudson's York & North Midland Railway Company had obtained an act to build a branch line between Bridlington, Filey and Seamer to join up with the York and Scarborough Railway which had opened on July 7th, 1845.

Although the Hull & Selby Company promoted the Hull - Bridlington line, due to it being leased to the York & North Midland from July 1st, 1845, the whole of the Hull - Bridlington - Scarborough line became part of George Hudson's Y & NM rail network.

The Hull and Bridlington Railway was originally planned for single line working, but it was completed as a double track railway by Messrs. Jackson & Bean who also installed the new electric telegraph system.

The Seamer Junction - Filey section was opened on October 5th, 1846 and the Hull - Bridlington line the following day. The Bridlington - Filey section opened on October 20th, 1847, thus completing the through connection between Hull and Scarborough.

Originally trains from Hull used the Company's Railway Street Station. The Bridlington branch left the Hull - Selby line at Dairycoates and turned northwards towards Cottingham. From 1848 passenger traffic was transferred to the new Paragon Station which was near to the city centre.

During 1947, the London & North Eastern Railway built a station to serve Butlin's Filey Holiday Camp. It was situated at the end of a small branch line from a double junction off the main lines between Hunmanby and Filey and was controlled by three signal boxes. These together with the station were manned be relief staff each summer Saturday when the Camp was open. The station was closed in 1977.

In an early spate of rural station closures, British Railways withdrew passenger services from the stations at Cayton 1952, Gristhorpe 1959 and Lockington 1960.

In the Beeching report on the reshaping of British Railways, it was proposed to modify the Hull - Scarborough line, with five intermediate stations recommended for closure. Then in 1966 it was announced that the Railways Board were thinking of closing the line. When British Railways announced their plans to axe the line in 1968, it brought about the biggest public outcry ever heard over a closure. At the resulting public enquiry there were 3,444 objections including those of 14 local authorities. It was stated that 2,892 people were known regular users of the daily service, with summer holiday trains carrying 88,000 passengers and excursions a further 108,000. This gave a total of 2,300,000 passenger journeys a year covering some 44,000,000 miles.

On July 29th, 1969 the Minister of Transport Mr Richard Marsh announced his decision to refuse consent to full closure of the line, but he agreed to the closure of Lowthorpe, Burton Agnes, Carnaby, Flamborough and Speeton. A full grant to keep the line operating was to be met by the Government.

In recent years measures have been taken to reduce operating costs. These include single line working between Bridlington – Hunmanby and Filey – Seamer Junction. The line had a large number of traditional manned level crossings. These have been replaced with automatic barriers and most of the stations reduced to unmanned halts. Since the 1980's Humberside County Council has provided grants to assist British Rail with improvements to the line.

About to leave Paragon station with the 8-30 am Hull - Bridlington - Scarborough service on July 9th, 1960, class B1 4-6-O No.61270 pilots the train locomotive, an unidentified D49 4-4-O. Heavily laden trains on this service needed to be double headed to work the steep section between Bridlington and Hunmanby. PHOTOGRAPH D. LOVEDAY (GRESLEY SOCIETY).

Locomotives of the D49 class were named after either County Shires or Hunts. On this occasion one of the Hunts engine No.62727 "The Quorn" passes Hymers College with a parcels train to Bridlington. PHOTOGRAPH NEVILLE STEAD.

55

Dairycoates shed class K3 2-6-O No.61941 at Cottingham South Junction passes the Ideal Standard sidings with a service train from Bridlington.
PHOTOGRAPH NEVILLE STEAD COLLECTION.

York class B1 4-6-O No.61084 calls at Cottingham with a York - Hull stopping train circa 1961. The service was worked alternately by steam engines and diesel rail cars. Cottingham has the distinction of being the largest village in England.
PHOTOGRAPH NEVILLE STEAD.

Two young train spotters note B16 4-6-O No.61454 as it passes Cottingham North signalbox with an evening Hull - York train during August 1959. Several B16's were allocated from York to Dairycoates in the class's twilight years.
PHOTOGRAPH NEVILLE STEAD.

Essential maintenance to the track is usually done from late on Saturday night through Sunday. A ballast train hauled by a Brush Type 2 (class 31) diesel electric locomotive, passes Beverley station signalbox as it heads south to the Hull yards on a Sunday engineering working.
PHOTOGRAPH MICHAEL CLARKE.

Station staff had an intense pride in their station and kept it clean and tidy. In summer the station gardens were a mass of colour with bedding plants as seen in this view of Beverley in 1964. The Railway Company was keen to encourage these activities and awarded prizes and certificates for the best kept gardens.
PHOTOGRAPH BY COURTESY OF THE YORKSHIRE POST.

Doncaster based K3 2-6-0 No.61800 heads north through Beverley station for York, with a train of empty flat wagons. The busy market town of Beverley has a fine Minster, the spires of which are seen above the water tank.
PHOTOGRAPH NEVILLE STEAD COLLECTION.

A view of Arram station facing north in May 1959. The station is close to R.A.F. Leconfield and over the years it was used by many of the servicemen and women who where based there. Before the Hull & Hornsea Railway was built there were plans for a line linking Hornsea to the Hull - Bridlington line at Arram. PHOTOGRAPH DOUGLAS THOMPSON.

A view of Lockington Station facing north. The station was closed to passengers in 1960. On July 26th, 1986 Lockington was the scene of a tragedy when a van was driven through the automatic level crossing into the path of the O9.33 Bridlington - Hull diesel multiple unit train, which was derailed and badly damaged. Sadly nine people were killed, eight of whom were passengers on the train. PHOTOGRAPH DOUGLAS THOMPSON.

Class V3 2-6-4 No.67663 arriving at Driffield station with an all stations stopping train to Bridlington. At the front of the train are two fish vans, a regular feature on this service. Driffield is a market town which serves the local farming community.
PHOTOGRAPH NEVILLE STEAD.

Nafferton has typical rural station buildings for the line, with station master's house, ticket office and waiting room in the main structure, and a coal yard, goods shed and a wooden shelter. The signalbox is now disused and has become a listed building. It is proposed that it can be moved to a preserved railway.
PHOTOGRAPH NEVILLE STEAD COLLECTION.

Class D49/2 4-4-O No.62756 "The Brocklesby" rattles the station fittings as it rushes through Carnaby station with a Scarborough - Hull stopping train (But not Carnaby).
PHOTOGRAPH TONY ROSS.

A spectacular display of power south of Bridlington as the driver and fireman of "Black Five" No.44929 put their charge to its task, working a return excursion from Bridlington to Huddersfield on Easter Monday April 19th, 1959.
PHOTOGRAPH TONY ROSS.

On a busy Sunday evening in the summer of 1958, the signalman at Carnaby watches as Stanier "Black Five" 4-6-O No.45035 heads homeward to the south through his block section.
PHOTOGRAPH TONY ROSS.

Class D11/1 4-4-O No.62662 "Prince of Wales" works south out of Bridlington station with a return working to Sheffield on Bank Holiday Monday, May 18th, 1959. Bridlington shed can be seen behind the signal gantry. PHOTOGRAPH NEVILLE STEAD.

The "Holiday maker" Inter City 125, Hull - Glasgow service via Bridlington - Filey - Scarborough - York - Newcastle and Edinburgh approaching Bridlington in July 1991. The carriage sidings on the left were used to store visiting excursion trains on busy Summer weekends.
PHOTOGRAPH TONY ROSS.

In this mid 1950's scene, K3 2-6-O No.61941 arrives at Bridlington platform 5 with a summer Saturday train from the direction of Filey. The station staff at this busy holiday resort were hard pressed looking after the welfare of the scores of holiday-makers and day-trippers passing through the station on summer weekends.
PHOTOGRAPH TONY ROSS.

B16 4-6-O No.61443 waits at Bridlington platform 2 heading north with the summer Saturday 9.05 am Liverpool exchange - Scarborough service in 1957. This train ran via Wigan, Bury, Rochdale, Wakefield, Castleford, Selby and Market Weighton. It had Liverpool Bank Hall motive power as far as Gascoigne Wood, Selby. The overall roof was removed in 1961 and the two platforms it covered are now part of a housing estate.
PHOTOGRAPH TONY ROSS.

Bridlington shed on a busy summer Saturday. Although the shed lost its allocation in June 1958 and was "closed" in the following December it still continued to service visiting excursion locomotives for some years afterwards.
PHOTOGRAPH NEVILLE STEAD.

Holiday-makers have to wait while WD 2-8-O No.90021 shunts Bridlington goods yard circa 1954. The yard is now the site of a Tesco store.
PHOTOGRAPH TONY ROSS.

Class WD 2-8-O No.90272 works south through Bridlington with the pick up freight to Hull inward yard on August 1st, 1964.
PHOTOGRAPH DOUG HARDY.

On the climb north of Bempton station class D49 4-4-O No.62770 "The Puckeridge" pilots Ivatt class 4 2-6-O No.43057 on a heavily laden 11 coach summer Saturday train. The nearby high cliffs at Bempton are home to a wide variety of seabirds and the whole area is consequently very popular with bird watchers.
PHOTOGRAPH NEVILLE STEAD.

Passing through the chalk cuttings north of Flamborough station, B16 4-6-O No.61445 on a 10 coach Gloucester - Filey Holiday Camp train attacks the 1 in 92 climb on the scenic section of line between Bridlington and Hunmanby.
PHOTOGRAPH TONY ROSS.

Heading south with a summer Saturday additional service in 1957. Leeds Holbeck shed Jubilee class 4-6-O engine No.45573
"Newfoundland" passes through Speeton station near to the summit of the line.
PHOTOGRAPH TONY ROSS.

Leaving Hunmanby and heading south up the gradient, British Railways Standard class 4 tank engine No.80119 of Whitby shed has been "borrowed" to work the 2.45 pm Scarborough - Hull stopping train in the summer of 1955. PHOTOGRAPH TONY ROSS.

One of the newly introduced English Electric Type 4 diesel electric locomotives, joins the main line at Royal Oak South with a Saturday only Filey Holiday Camp train in the summer of 1959. The Butlin's Filey Holiday Camp was once a very popular spot for family holidays. But in the 1970's this type of holiday went into decline. The last train to the camp ran on September 17th, 1977 and on November 26th, closure of the station was announced. The derelict camp site is now being demolished. PHOTOGRAPH TONY ROSS.

In August 1955, at the popular family resort of Filey holiday-makers rush for a seat on a south bound express passenger train, worked by B1 4-6-0 No.61145. This station which still has its overall roof was recently repainted in the old North Eastern Railway chocolate and cream livery. PHOTOGRAPH J.W. ARMSTRONG.

Botanic Gardens shed D49 4-4-0 No.62720 "Cambridgeshire" calls at Seamer station with a Scarborough - Hull, all stations (except Carnaby and Lockington) stopping train in the summer of 1949. PHOTOGRAPH W.A. CAMWELL.

Preserved class K4 2-6-O "The Great Marquess" pilots class K1 2-6-O No.62005 through Carnaby station with the S.L.S. Whitby Moors railtour on March 6th, 1965. This was a sad occasion as the railtour ran over the doomed Whitby - Scarborough and Goathland - Pickering lines which closed on March 8th, 1965.
PHOTOGRAPH DOUG HARDY.

HULL TO SCARBOROUGH

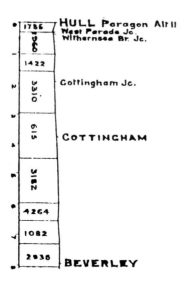

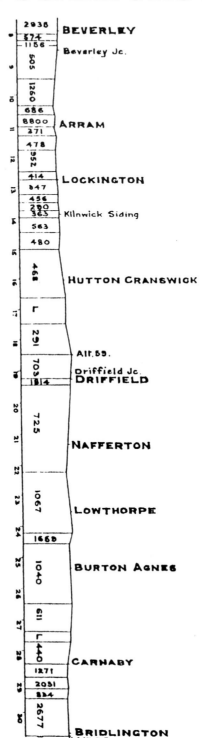

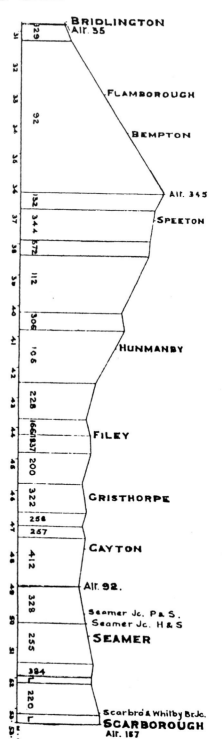

Table 25—continued

HULL, BRIDLINGTON, FILEY and SCARBOROUGH

SATURDAYS ONLY

				D			K	G			H	L	L	L		J	E	Z	J	F	G	N	M	P		L
				Leeds dep 8.0 am		Mkt.Weighton dep 9.10 am	Sheffield (Vic.) dep 7.12 am	Rotherham (Central) dep 7.47 am	Selby dep 9.20 am		Leeds dep 9.15 am	Sheffield (Vic.) dep 8.36 am	Leeds dep 9.28 am	Bradford (Ex.) dep 8.55 am	Chesterfield (Mid) dep 8.20 am	Stalybridge dep 8.55 am	York dep 10.38 am		Manchester (Ex.) dep 9.0 am	Leicester (Cen.) dep 8b25 am	Sowerby Bridge dep 9.50 am	Silkstone dep 9.58 am	Sheffield (Vic.) dep 10.30 am			Refreshment Car from King's Cross
16 London (King's Cross) dep	pm 11 45	am	am	am	am	am	am	am 3 50	am	am	am	am	am	am	am	am	am	noon 3 50	am	pm	pm	pm	pm	pm	pm	am 8 20
HULL dep	am 5 30	5 55	7 38	8 35	…	9 0	…	…	…	…	10 10	…	…	…	…	10 35	…	11 25	…	…	…	…	…	…	12 20	…	pm …
Cottingham	…	…	…	…	…	…	…	…	…	…	…	…	…	…	…	10 44	…	…	…	…	…	…	…	…	12 28	…	…
Beverley arr	…	…	7 46	8 44	…	9 12	…	…	…	…	10 19	…	…	…	…	10 51	…	11 39	…	…	…	…	…	…	12 35	…	…
Beverley dep	…	…	7 53	8 51	…	9 16	…	…	…	…	10 26	…	…	…	…	10 54	…	11 41	…	…	…	…	…	…	12 36	…	…
Arram	5 49	…	8 1	…	…	…	…	…	…	…	10 28	…	…	…	…	11 0	…	…	…	…	…	…	…	…	…	…	…
Lockington	…	6 15	8 6	…	…	…	…	…	…	…	…	…	…	…	…	…	…	…	…	…	…	…	…	…	…	…	…
Hutton Cranswick	…	6 21	8 12	…	…	…	…	…	…	…	…	…	…	…	…	…	…	…	…	…	…	…	…	…	…	…	…
Driffield arr	6 16	6 27	8 18	9 9	…	…	…	…	…	…	10 32	10 34	…	…	…	10 43	10 45	…	…	…	…	…	…	…	12 52	…	…
Driffield dep	6 17	6 33	8 20	9 11	…	…	…	…	…	…	10 40	…	…	…	…	…	…	…	…	…	…	…	…	…	12 53	…	…
Nafferton	…	6 38	8 26	…	…	…	…	…	…	…	10 46	…	…	…	…	…	…	…	…	…	…	…	…	…	…	…	…
Lowthorpe	…	6 43	8 31	…	…	…	…	…	…	…	…	…	…	…	…	…	…	…	…	…	…	…	…	…	…	…	…
Burton Agnes	…	6 51	8 35	…	…	…	…	…	…	…	…	…	…	…	…	…	…	…	…	…	…	…	…	…	…	…	…
Carnaby	6 17	…	8 41	…	…	…	…	…	…	…	…	…	…	…	…	…	…	…	…	…	…	…	…	…	…	…	…
Bridlington arr	6 25	6 56	8 46	9 27	9 35	9 46	9 55	10 3	10 10	10 54	11 1	11 7	11 13	11 21	11 29	11 36	11 44	11 51	12 0	12 18	12 25	12 33	12 41	12 50	1 2	1 9	1 16
Bridlington dep	6 35	…	8 51	9 30	…	9 51	…	…	…	11 4	…	…	11D26	…	…	11 41	11 49	11 57	12 5	…	12 30	12 38	12 47	12 56	1 7	…	1 21
Flamborough	6 46	…	8 58	…	…	…	…	…	…	11 11	…	…	…	…	…	…	…	…	…	…	…	…	…	…	…	…	…
Bempton	…	…	9 4	…	…	…	…	…	…	11 17	…	…	…	…	…	…	…	…	…	…	…	…	…	…	…	…	…
Speeton	…	…	9 13	…	…	…	…	…	…	…	…	…	…	…	…	…	…	…	…	…	…	…	…	…	…	…	…
Hunmanby	6 59	…	9 21	…	…	…	…	…	…	11 30	…	…	…	…	…	…	…	…	…	…	…	…	…	…	1 31	…	1 43
Filey Holiday Camp arr	…	…	…	…	9 52	…	…	…	…	…	…	…	11D49	…	…	…	…	12 29	…	…	12 53	…	…	…	…	1 31	…
Filey arr	7 4	…	9 26	9 52	…	10 13	…	…	…	11 35	…	…	12 3	12 13	12 23	…	…	…	…	…	12 53	1 0	1 10	1 20	…	…	…
Filey dep	7 11	…	9 31	…	…	10 17	…	…	…	11 37	…	…	12 5	12 17	12 27	…	…	…	…	…	…	1 5	1 15	1 25	…	…	…
Gristhorpe	…	…	9 36	…	…	…	…	…	…	…	…	…	…	…	…	…	…	…	…	…	…	…	…	…	…	…	…
Seamer	7 26	…	9 46	…	…	…	…	…	…	11 49	…	…	…	…	…	…	…	…	…	…	…	…	…	…	…	…	…
SCARBOROUGH (C) Londesborough Road arr	…	…	…	…	…	…	…	…	…	…	…	…	12 34	12 42	…	…	…	…	…	…	…	…	1 23	1 30	1 45	…	…
Central	7 32	…	9 52	…	…	10 35	…	…	…	11 55	…	…	12 20	…	…	…	…	…	…	…	…	…	…	…	…	…	…
27 Middlesbrough arr	…	…	11 4	…	…	2 37	…	…	…	…	…	…	3c46	…	…	…	…	…	…	…	…	…	…	…	…	…	…
28 York	…	9 3	11 22	…	…	12L14	…	…	…	…	…	…	1 42	…	…	…	…	…	…	…	…	…	…	…	…	…	…

A—For complete service between Hull and Beverley see Table 18.
B—For other trains from Seamer to Scarborough see Table 28.
C—600 yards between Londesborough Road and Central Stations.
D—Runs 4th July to 5th September inclusive.
E—Runs 11th July to 15th August inclusive.
F—Not after 29th August.
G—Runs 20th June to 12th September inclusive.
H—Runs 4th July to 12th September inclusive.
J—Runs 4th July to 29th August inclusive.
K—Runs 20th June to 22nd August inclusive.
L—Not after 12th September.
M—Runs 20th June to 5th September inclusive.
N—Runs 27th June to 22nd August inclusive.
P—Not after 5th September.
Z—Not after 12th September. On 13th, 20th and 27th June and 12th September starts at Leeds (City) (depart 10.0 am).
b—Departs Leicester (Central) 7.45 am on 20th and 27th June, also 5th and 12th September.
c—Runs 18th July to 22nd August inclusive.

Table 25—continued

HULL, BRIDLINGTON, FILEY and SCARBOROUGH

		SATURDAYS ONLY—continued																			SUNDAYS					
		E		**H**	**H**	**F**	**H**			**F**		**J**															
		pm	pm	pm	pm	pm	pm	pm	am 9 10	pm	am 10 35	pm	pm	pm	pm 12P35	pm 1L30		pm	pm 2 18	pm 3D50			am 11p45	am	am	am 10 10	pm 1 18
16 London (King's Cross) dep		..	..	..	..	..	..																				
HULL .... dep			12 45					1 20	2 25 pm		3 42 pm			4 25	5 45	6 49		8 15	9 45	....			8 30	10 20		11 40	5 40	6 50
Cottingham ...... arr	A		12 58					1 29	2 34		3 50			4 34	5 54	6 58		8 24	9 54	....			8 39	10 29		11 49	5 49	6 59
Beverley .... dep			12 59					1 36	2 41		3 57			4 41	6 1	7 5		8 31	10 1	....			8 46	10 36		11 56	5 56	7 6
Arram .... "								1 44	2 44		3 59			4 43	6 3	7 7		8 32	10 2				8 49	10 39		11 58	5 58	7 8
Lockington .... "								1 50						4 49	6 9	..		8 38	10 8				8 54	..		..	..	..
Hutton Cranswick arr								1 55						4 54	6 14	..		8 43	10 13				..	..		..	..	..
Driffield .... dep			1 15					2 1						5 2	6 20	..		8 50	10 20				9 4	..		..	..	..
			1 16					2 7	2 58	3 30	4 13			5 10	6 26	7 22	7 36	8 55	10 25				9 10	10 54		12 13	6 13	7 23
Nafferton .... "								2 12	3 0	3 31	4 15			5 13	6 29	7 24	7 37	8 56	10 27				9 12	10 56		12 15	6 15	7 25
Lowthorpe .... "								2 17						5 18	6 34	..		9 2	10 32							12 21		
Burton Agnes .... "								2 22						5 23	6 39	..		9 7	10 37									
Carnaby .... "														5 27	6 44	..		9 12	10 42									
														5 33	6 50	..		9 18	10 48									
Bridlington ...... arr		1 24	1 33	1 50	1 58	2 8	2 18	2 33	3 16	3 47	4 31	4 40	5 38	6 54	7 40	7 53	9 22	10 53				9 28	11 11	11 47	12 33	6 30	7 40
dep		1 29	1 38	1 55	2 5	2 15	2 23	2 38	3 21		4 34	4 45		7 1								9 31	11 18			6 35	
Flamborough .. "			1 46								4 40			7 7												6 42	
Bempton .... "			1 51					2 48			4 45			7 13												6 47	
Speeton.. .. "											4 53			7 20												6 55	
Hunmanby .... "								N	3 41		4 59			7 26												7 2	
Filey Holiday Camp arr		1 52	2 8	2 18	2 28	2 38	2 45	3 6	3 46		5 4	5 7		7 31												7 7	
Filey .... dep			2 11	2 23	2 33	2 43		3 9	3 50		5 7			7 34								9 53	11 40			7 9	
Gristhorpe ...... "								N			N											9 55	11 42				
Scamer .... "								3 20	4 1		5 7			7 46												7 21	
SCARBOROUGH (C) arr	B																					10 7	11 54				
Londesborough Road "			2 29	2 37	2 47	2 57		3 26	4 9		5 21			7 52								10 13	12 0			7 29	
Central																											
27 Middlesbrough .. arr		5K36				6b48	7 28		8G40														11M37	3 26		10 25	
28 York .... "		4Y28	5 19			6K52				9Y 4															8Y28		

Vertical notes in columns: Worcester (S.H.) dep 7.15 am / Liverpool (Ex.) dep 9.5 am / Manchester (London Rd.) dep 10.0 am / Basford & Bulwell 9.40 am / Newcastle dep 10.25 am / Leeds (City) dep 1.29 pm / York dep 3.30 pm / Selby dep 6.20 pm / Through Carriage—London (King's Cross) to Bridlington / Leeds dep 10.0 am

---

A—For complete service between Hull and Beverley see Table 18.
B—For other trains from Seamer to Scarborough see Table 28.
C—600 yards between Londesborough Road and Central Stations.

D—Passengers can depart King's Cross 5.30 pm by Pullman Car train (Supplementary charges).
E—Not after 5th September.
F—Runs 4th July to 29th August inclusive.
G—Runs 20th June to 22nd August inclusive.
H—Not after 29th August.

J—Not after 12th September.
K—Runs 4th July to 12th September inclusive.
L—Runs 27th June to 12th September inclusive.
M—Until 12th July inclusive and on 13th and 20th September arrives York 11.42 am.

N—Calls when required.
P—Runs 27th June to 29th August.
SH—Shrub Hill.
Y—Connection at Seamer.
b—Runs 18th July to 22nd August inclusive.
p—pm.

THE CROSS COUNTRY WOLD LINES

By 1846, the East Riding was encompassed by railways which were either completed or under construction. These were controlled by George Hudson's York & North Midland Railway Company. However the rich agricultural central area was not served by rail and it was here that other companies were looking to gain access.

Captain Laws of the Manchester & Leeds Railway Company had ambitions for his company to control a network of railways linking the West and East coasts. He conceived a scheme to build two new lines, one from Leeds to York and a second from York to Hull, thus bypassing the existing Leeds - Selby - Hull route.

A further threat of competition came from the proposed York, Hull, East & West Yorkshire Railway Company which planned to build a line joining Scarborough, Bridlington, Driffield, Market Weighton and Howden.

George Hudson's reaction to these proposals was a brilliant piece of strategy. In 1845 he bought Londesborough Park, an estate of 12,000 acres, from the 6th Duke of Devonshire for £470,000. As the estate covered the best area through which a York to Hull line would pass he had effectively blocked his opponent's schemes.

The York & North Midland Railway Company promoted its own lines from York to Beverley and Selby to Market Weighton. These were authorised by separate acts on June 18th 1846. Opposition to the bill from the local canal owners was overcome by buying them out at inflated prices. The railway then took over the Pocklington, Market Weighton and Leven canals under an act of 1847.

THE YORK - MARKET WEIGHTON - BEVERLEY LINE

The Y & NM's proposed York - Market Weighton - Beverley line was completed only as far as Market Weighton. Built as double track it was opened on October 4th, 1847 and cost £380,000 to build.

The Market Weighton - Beverley section fell victim to a spell of railway recession and problems with local landowners. Although the line terminated at Market Weighton it still proved profitable.

On July 31st, 1854 the North Eastern Railway Company was formed and it took over the line. The newly formed NER soon found itself being requested for the link to Hull via Beverley to be completed. Work on the Market Weighton - Beverley line began in 1862, following tough bargaining with Lord Hotham of Dalton whose estate most of the line passed. One of the conditions was that of a station being built at Kipling Coates to serve his nearby estate and another was that no trains ran on a Sunday. The line was opened to traffic on May 1st 1865. Originally built as single track it was doubled in 1889.

Following the opening of this new railway link with York via Beverley, the weekday Hull - York passenger service which had previously worked via Selby was transferred to the new route. The Sunday service remained via Selby. Freight traffic from the north was worked via both Selby and Beverley.

In a spate of pre-war closures the L.N.E.R. closed the station at Holtby on September 9th, 1939. Then in a pre-Beeching bout of station closures British Railways closed Nunburnholme on March 31st, 1951 followed by Cherry Burton, Fangfoss and Warthill all on January 3rd, 1959. In 1953 Warthill had the distinction of being the first British station to have its level crossing fitted with lifting barriers.

On December 17th, 1959 British Railways announced that the first system of centralised traffic control in this country was to be installed on the 34 mile long York - Beverley line. Under the plan long stretches of line could be controlled by one signal box. The route was to be singled, with passing loops at Market Weighton and Pocklington. Traditional manually operated level crossings were to be modernised with automatic barriers activated by the trains, the whole route being controlled from York.

The scheme, which was estimated to cost £83,000, was predicted to pay for itself by way of reduced operating costs within 7 years. After this time the line was expected to run at a profit of around £6,000 per year.

By 1962, the Government's attitude to transport had changed with a move away from railways in favour of road transport. Although some preliminary work had been carried out on the York - Beverley modernisation scheme the plan was scrapped following the change of attitude. Then in 1963 the line was listed for closure under the Beeching economy plan.

A public meeting was held at Pocklington on July 7th, 1964

where the Transport Users Consultative Committee heard objections against the line's closure. Following strong opposition from the East Riding County Council, the Yorkshire & Humberside Economic Consultative Planning Council, local schools and the general public, the TUCC advised the Minister of hardship if the line were to be closed.

With the departure of Dr. Beeching during May 1965, back to his old post at I.C.I. there were hopes that the Minister of Transport in the new Labour Government, Tom Fraser, would move to save the line, but to the dismay of all concerned on August 3rd, 1965 he consented to the closure of the line.

On the last day of service November 27th 1965, the Hull based class B1 4-6-0 No.61306 was used on locomotive hauled workings and a 6 car DMU operated the final 21.42 pm train from York.

THE SELBY - MARKET WEIGHTON - DRIFFIELD LINE

The Y & NMR's Selby - Market Weighton line, which was constructed as a single track railway opened on August 8th, 1848 and cost £156,000 to build. This rural branch line was built for its strategic rather than financial value. The NER took over the line on July 31st, 1854.

The Selby - Market Weighton line's potential was greatly increased when in 1890 the Scarborough, Bridlington & West Junction Railway opened its line between Driffield and Market Weighton thus providing a through route from Selby to the coastal resorts of Bridlington, Filey and Scarborough for traffic from West Yorkshire and the Midlands. The Driffield - Market Weighton Line opened for freight on April 18th, 1890 and passenger traffic on May 1st.

In anticipation of increased traffic the new through route would create, the NER converted the Selby - Market Weighton line to double track from July 1st, 1890. At the same time the remote station at Duffield Gate was closed.

In its early years of operating the line British Railways provided a similar service to that of the L.N.E.R. This consisted of 2 stopping trains in each direction on weekdays, but as costs increased the Government's attitude to the railways providing a loss making rural service changed and stations were closed. Low passenger receipts from the intermediate stations of the Bridlington - Selby service soon came under scrutiny, resulting in the closure of Cliffe Common, Bubwith, Highfield, Foggathorpe, Holme Moor, Everingham, Enthorpe, Middleton on the Wolds, Bainton and Southburn, on September 18th, 1954. Menthorpe Gate was closed on December 5th, 1953.

Although the Selby - Driffield line continued to be used by excursion traffic to the coastal resorts, it was realised that this traffic could be diverted via the Selby - Hull - Bridlington lines. So when Dr. Beeching published his reshaping report in May 1963 the Selby - Driffield line was an obvious target for closure.

Following the usual public meeting, the Transport Users Consultative Committee reported their findings to the Minister of Transport, Tom Fraser, who gave his consent to closure in the notice of withdrawal on February 26th, 1965.

The last regular service train between Bridlington - Driffield - Market Weighton - Selby ran on June 12th, 1965. The final double journey was made by an 8 coach train, which left Bridlington at 7.35 am and returned at 10.28 am. Almost 200 passengers made the last trip, most of whom were railway enthusiasts. The line closed completely on June 14th, 1965.

English Electric Type 4 diesel electric locomotive No.282 passes through Cherry Burton station with a York - Hull train on June 10th 1965, a few months before the closure of the line. The once well cared for rural station is showing signs of neglect having closed to passengers on January 5th, 1959.
PHOTOGRAPH D.P. LECKONBY.

Class D16/3 4-4-0 engine No.62571 with an R.C.T.S. East Midlander railtour between Cherry Burton and Kipling Coates on Sunday May 12th, 1957. The tour which started from Nottingham, ran via Chesterfield and Rotherham to Cudworth to travel over the Hull & Barnsley, then onto the Albert and St. Andrew's Docks at Hull, then to York via Market Weighton. Returning home via Selby, Doncaster, Maltby, Shireoaks, Elmton and Mansfield to Nottingham. PHOTOGRAPH CECIL ORD COLLECTION.

An unidentified WD 2-8-0 running tender first with a Hull - York freight near to Kipling Coates on May 6th, 1965. Running wrong way round was unpopular with footplate crews because of the draught and coal dust blown into the cab. PHOTOGRAPH DOUG HARDY.

A view of Kipling Coates station facing east with a diesel railcar train on the York - Hull service about to leave for its next stop at Beverley. Although this rural station was a prime candidate for closure in the 1959 pre-Beeching bout of station closures, British Railways were obliged to keep the station open to serve Lord Hotham's estate. PHOTOGRAPH D.P. LECKONBY.

The west end of Market Weighton station, where the lines from York and Selby converged. The station was the busy cross roads for Hull - York and Selby - Driffield - Bridlington trains. PHOTOGRAPH NEVILLE STEAD COLLECTION.

Pocklington station looking towards Market Weighton circa 1949. Designed by G.T. Andrews the station had an overall roof, a feature of all the York & North Midland Railway stations which served the larger communities. After closure the end portions of the station were bricked in to make a gymnasium for the use of Pocklington School and the local public. PHOTOGRAPH DOUGLAS THOMPSON.

Stamford Bridge looking towards Market Weighton circa 1949. Stamford Bridge was one of the few stations in the area to retain its original name. This was possibly due to the historic importance of the village. At the northern end of the station a fine viaduct (which still stands) carried the line over the River Derwent. PHOTOGRAPH DOUGLAS THOMPSON.

Class D49 4-4-O No.62754 "The Berkeley" with a York - Hull train near Holtby in 1949. The rural station at Holtby was closed by the L.N.E.R. in 1939. PHOTOGRAPH CECIL ORD COLLECTION.

Class B16 4-6-O No.61435 heads south through York station with a freight train for Hull yard via Selby. On the left class J71 O-6-O tank No.68297 is on station pilot duties. PHOTOGRAPH AUTHOR'S COLLECTION.

A Derby shed, Stanier "Black Five" 4-6-0 mixed traffic engine No.44856 passes through Cliff Common station with a summer Saturday 8.20 am Chesterfield - Scarborough train. Cliff Common was closed to passengers from September 20th, 1954 and for goods from January 27th, 1964. The station was linked to the southern end of the Derwent Valley Light Railway.
PHOTOGRAPH J.F. SEDGWICK.

Working the summer Saturday 8.30 am Manchester Exchange - Filey Holiday Camp train, Class B16 4-6-0 No.61471 taking advantage of the flat section of track between Selby and Market Weighton speeds past Duffield Gate station buildings. This rural station was closed as early as 1890, the year the North Eastern Railway converted the line to double track.
PHOTOGRAPH J.F. SEDGWICK.

A view of the railway junction at the eastern end of Market Weighton. Leeds Neville Hill class K1 2-6-0 engine No.62007 having passed Market Weighton East signalbox is heading for Bridlington via Driffield. The track on the left led to Beverley.
PHOTOGRAPH TONY ROSS.

British Railways Standard class 5 4-6-O engine No.73069 attacks the 1 in 95 climb on the section between Market Weighton and Enthorpe, with a Bank Holiday Monday Rotherham Masborough - Bridlington train on August 3rd, 1959.
PHOTOGRAPH NEVILLE STEAD.

Close to the summit of the line trains passed through the chalk cutting at Enthorpe. This was a very popular venue for train spotters on summer Saturdays. The varied selection of motive power pressed into service on the coastal holiday trains, the sight of engines at work on the climb and the sound echoing off the cutting walls will live on in many peoples memories. On this occasion D49 No.62770 "The Puckeridge" pilots Ivatt class 4 No.43057 (flying pig), with a Sowerby Bridge - Scarborough train on August 22nd, 1959. As usual the pilot engine appears to be doing all the work.
PHOTOGRAPH NEVILLE STEAD.

A view of the main station buildings at Middleton on the Wolds. The goods yard and coal cells were situated to the rear. The stations at Enthorpe, Bainton, and Southburn were of a similar design.
PHOTOGRAPH AUTHOR'S COLLECTION.

To the south west of Driffield, the line from Selby joined the Malton - Driffield Branch line at Driffield West junction. This in turn lead to the junction with the Hull - Bridlington line onto which Black Five No.44932 is heading north with a Sunday excursion Charlston - Bridlington train on July 12th, 1959.
PHOTOGRAPH AUTHOR'S COLLECTION.

SELBY TO DRIFFIELD

YORK TO HULL

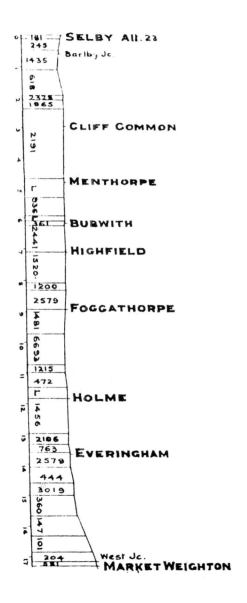

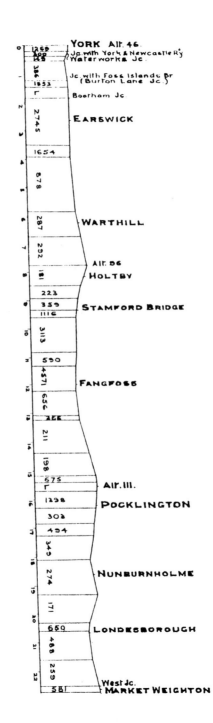

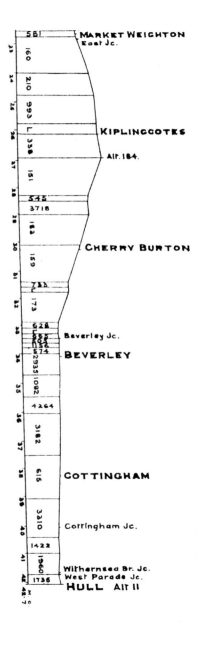

YORK AND HULL
23rd MAY to 25th SEPTEMBER, 1949

Table 18

WEEKDAYS / SUNDAYS (Down: Newcastle, Darlington, York → Hull)

Station	am	am	am	am	am (Filey, arr 12.1 pm)	am/pm (SO)	am	pm	pm	pm (Filey SO, arr 4.33 pm)	pm (SO)	pm	pm	pm	pm	pm	pm	**Sun** am	am	pm	pm	pm	pm
Newcastle ... dep	1 24	2 29		8 5		8 5	8 32	10 0	10 0		1 q 1	1 26	2 35	2 35	4 31	5 0	7 30	6 52	1045	2 45	3 10	7 10	7 30
Darlington ... ,,	12a21	3 26	6 20	9 5		9 5	9 32	10 50	1050		1 34	2 23	3 38	3 38	5 22	6 1	8 36	8 12	1137	3 11	4 10	8 19	8 36
YORK ... dep	3 40	7 55	8 20	10 10		10 20	10 45	12 15	1225		2 55	3 25	5 5	5 22	6 25	7 15	9 55	9 42	1231	4 20	7 15	9 38	9 55
Earswick ,,		8 1						12 21						5 28									
Warthill ,,		8 8						12 28						5 35									
Stamford Bridge ,,		8 15						12 35				3 40		5 42		7 30							
Fangfoss ,,		8 20						12 40						5 47									
Pocklington ,,		8 31		10 32				12 49				3 51	5 27	5 56		7 41	1017						
Nunburnholme ,,		8 36						12 54						6 1									
Londesborough ,,		8 41						12 59						6 6									
Market Weighton arr		8 45		10 42				1 3				4 1	5 37	6 10		7 51	1027						
Bridlington arr		9n35		1B16	11 32		2B36			4 5	5B38		6B54	7 40		9B27							
Market Weighton dep		8 47		10 43				1 5				4 2	5 38	6 12		7 52	1028						
Kipling Cotes ,,		8 54						1 12						6 19									
Cherry Burton ,,		9 1						1 19						6 28									
Beverley {arr}		9 8	11 1					1 25				4 20	5 56	6 34		8 9	1046						
Beverley {dep}		9 11	11 2					1 28				4 22	5 58	6 36		8 10	1047						
Cottingham ,,		9 18	11 9					1 35				4 29		6 44		8 17	1054						
HULL ... arr	5 11	9 26	9 45	11 17		1k5		1 44	2g51		4 37		6 10	6 52	7 59	8 25	11 2	1142	5 6	10 9	9 45	11 5	11 5

Route annotations (Down): col 1 *Via Church Fenton and Selby*; cols 2–3 *Via Selby*; Filey columns *Through Train—York to Filey Holiday Camp (arr 12.1 pm / arr 4.33 pm)*; col 9 *Via Selby*; col 11 *Buffet Car*; col 17 *Via Selby*. Sundays: *Via Selby*, *Via Mickiefield and Selby*, *Through Train—York to Hull Via Church Fenton and Selby*, *Via Selby*.
A — Beverley / Cottingham group.

WEEKDAYS / SUNDAYS (Up: Hull → York, Darlington, Newcastle)

Station	am	am	am	H SO am	am	SO	G SO am	am	pm	pm	pm	pm	pm	pm	SX pm	SO pm	**Sun** am	pm	pm	pm	pm
HULL ... dep	5 35	7 0	7 55		9 40		1030	10 55	12 15	3 0	4 0	5 15	7 10	7 33	8 40	10 15	8 45	3 40	6 45	7 0	8 40
Cottingham ,,		7 8	8 3		9 48						4 10	5 24		7 41		10 24					
Beverley {arr}		7 15	8 10		9 55		1042		12 27	3 12	4 17	5 31		7 48		10 31					
Beverley {dep}		7 18	8 11		9 57		1043		12 29	3 14	4 19	5 32		7 51		10 32					
Cherry Burton ,,		7 26			10 5						4 27			8 0		10 40					
Kipling Cotes ,,		7 34			10 13						4 35			8 8		10 48					
Market Weighton arr		7 40	8 27		10 19				12 46	3 30	4 41	5 48		8 15		10 54					
Bridlington dep	6B30	7 45		9 32	8B22	10 12			11E0	1B55	3C45	4 S0	7 0								
Market Weighton dep		7 44	8 29		10 20				12 48	3 31	4 43	5 49		8 22							
Londesborough ,,		7 48			10 24						4 47			8 26							
Nunburnholme ,,		7 53			10 29						4 52			8 31							
Pocklington ,,		8 0	8 39		10 35				1 0	3 42	4 58	6 0		8 38							
Fangfoss ,,		8 8			10 41				1 8		5 6			8 46							
Stamford Bridge ,,		8 14			10 49				1 14		5 12			8 52							
Warthill ,,		8 21			10 56						5 19			8 59							
Earswick ,,		8 27			11 2				1 25		5 25			9 5							
YORK ... arr	7 13	8 33	8 58	10 50	11 11	11 19	1130	12 21	1 31		5 31	6 20	8 40	9 11		12a32	10 9	5 25	7 55	8 45	10 9
Darlington ... arr	9 42		10j11	12 14	12 14		1227	2h6	2 57	5 6		8f15		10 36	2a6		1125	7 22	9 21	9 40	11 28
Newcastle ... ,,	10j46		11j1	1 3	1 3		1 18	2h58	3 31	5 59		9f13		11b35	2a28		1231	8 39		1040	12a21

Route annotations (Up): col 1 *Via Selby*; H-column *Through Train—Filey Holiday Camp (dep 9.0 am) to York*; SO-column *Through Train—Filey Holiday Camp (dep 9.45 am) to York*; G SO-column *Through Train—Hull to Edinburgh (arr 4.27 pm)*; *Via Selby*; *Buffet Car*; Sundays col 4 *Through Train—Hull to York Via Selby and Church Fenton*; *Via Selby*.

A—For complete service between Hull and Beverley see Sheet NE 7   **B**—*Via Beverley*   **C**—Saturdays excepted. On Saturdays leaves Bridlington 3.26 pm *via Beverley*   **E**—*Via Beverley*. On Saturdays leaves Bridlington 11.15 am   **G**—Runs Saturdays 25th June to 3rd September inclusive   **H**—Runs 28th May, 4th June and 24th September   **S or SO**—Saturdays only   **a**—am   **b**—On Saturdays arrives Newcastle 11.42 pm   **f**—On Fridays (also Saturdays commencing 18th June) arrives Darlington 7.55 pm and Newcastle 8.53 pm   **g**—On Saturdays arrives Hull 1.51 pm   **h**—On Saturdays 11th June to 10th September inclusive arrives Darlington 1.36 pm and Newcastle 2.29 pm   **j**—On Mondays and Saturdays arrives Newcastle 10.43 am   **k**—On Saturdays arrives Hull 1.1 pm   **n**—On Saturdays arrives Bridlington 9.45 am   **p**—pm   **q**—Commencing 11th June leaves Newcastle 1.10 pm

SELBY MARKET WEIGHTON
DRIFFIELD AND BRIDLINGTON
23rd MAY to 25th SEPTEMBER, 1949

Table 25

WEEKDAYS — **SUNS.**

	SX am	B	SO	E	am	SO	D	am	SO	F	E	C	E	G	H	J	J	C	H	SO am	pm	SX am
Newcastle ... dep					2 29															10 0	1d26	6 52
Darlington ... ,,					6,20															10 50	2d23	8 12
York ... ,,					8,20															12 25	4 40	9 42
Leeds (City) ... dep	...	7 50			8 25	9 10			9 2½			10 40								1p35	5 13	10 25
SELBY ... dep					9 20			10 8												2 30	6 8	11 5
Cliff Common ... ,,					9 27															2 37	6 15	
Menthorpe Gate ... ,,					9 31															2 41	6 19	
Bubwith ... ,,					9 35															2 45	6 24	
High Field ... ,,					9 38															2 48	6 27	
Foggathorpe ... ,,					9 42															2 52	6 30	
Holme Moor ... ,,					9 48															2 58	6 37	
Everingham ... ,,					9 53															3 3	6 43	
Market Weighton ... arr					9 59			10 33												3 9	6 48	11 30
Newcastle ... dep	2 29			2 29			2 29														2 35	
Darlington ... ,,	3 26			3 26			3 26													1 34	3 38	
York ... ,,	7 55			7 55			7 55			10 20										2 55	5 22	
Market Weighton ... dep	8 55		9 5		10 2			10 35												3 11	6 53	11 32
Enthorpe ...					10 11															3 26	7 8	
Middleton-on-the-Wolds ...					10 17															3 30	7 12	
Bainton ...					10 21															3 35	7 17	
Southburn ...					10 26															3 41	7 19	
Driffield ... arr	9 17		9 28		10 32			11 0												3 42	7 24	
Driffield ... dep	9 19		9 30		10 34															3 42	7 24	
BRIDLINGTON ... arr	9 35	9 37	9 45	10 16	10 54	11 7	11 13	11 18	11 32	11 51	12 1	12 20	12 36	12 45	12 53	1 22	1 46	1 58		3 58	7 40	12 10
Filey ... arr		10 18	10 18		12R17	12 17	12 17	12 17	12 17	12 38				1 40		2 13	2 22	2 30	4B55	5T 4		
Scarborough (Cent.) ... ,,		10 39	10 39		12R38	12 38	12 38	12 38		12Z45	1Z25	1Z25	1Z47		2 31	2 31	2 45	2Z58	5B13	5T22		

WEEKDAYS — **SUNS.**

	MO am	N	K	SO	K	SO	H	H	SO	E	P	P	H	D	B	E	Q	G	G	SX	SO	pm	SX	pm
Scarborough (Cent.) dep		8 15	8 53	8 53	8 53	10Z15	10Z50		11 29	12 36	1 15	1 24		2 45	2 57	12 15	12 15	2U35	4V20	6 29	6 0			
Filey ... dep		8 30	9 11	9 11	9 11	10 33	11 8		12 36		1 24	1 24		2 36		12 55	2U55	4V4l	6 47	6 22				
BRIDLINGTON ... dep	7 0	7 45	9 32	9 58	10 12	10 38	10 50	11	7 11 35	12 40	1 25	1 42	2 12	2 20	2 30	3 3	3 35	3 44	3 45	7 0	7 50		8 35	
Driffield ... arr	7 22	7 59										4 16		7 14	8 4	4 1	4 16	7 17	8 6					
Driffield ... dep	7 25	8 0										4 24		7 23	8 14	4 9	4 24	7 29	8 14					
Southburn ...	7 31													7 24	8 14	4 15		7 29						
Bainton ...	7 37													7 29		4 19		7 34	8 17					
Middleton-on-the-Wolds ...	7 41															4 26	4 41	7 40						
Enthorpe ...	7 48															4 32	4 47	7 46						
Market Weighton ... arr	7 54	8 20															8 28		9 13					
York ... arr		8 58														5 31	9 11	9 11	10 36					
Darlington ... ,,		10 11														8e15	8e15	11f35						
Newcastle ... ,,		11 11														9el3	9el3							
Market Weighton ... dep	7 56															4 35	4 50	7 53	8 30	9 15				
Everingham ...	8 2															4 42	4 56	7 59						
Holme Moor ...	8 7															4 48	5 1	8 4						
Foggathorpe ...	8 13															4 55	5 7	8 14						
High Field ...	8 17															5 7	5 13	8 18						
Bubwith ...	8 20															5 11	5 18	8 23						
Menthorpe Gate ...	8 24															5 16	5 24	8 31						
Cliff Common ...	8 29															5 20	5 30	8 35						
SELBY ... arr	8 36															5 24	5 32	8 36	8 55	9 40				
Leeds (City) ... dep		9 35					1 48				3 0					6 24	6 24	9S32	9 38	10 23				
York ... arr		9 5					12 31									6 18	6 18							
Darlington ... ,,		10 11														8e15	8e15							
Newcastle ... ,,		11 1														9el3	9el3							

THE MALTON - DRIFFIELD RAILWAY

passenger service, although trains were used at times to provide transport for stranded villagers and the occasional scenic excusion. From 1955 the stone traffic ended and eventually the goods traffic dwindled so that in April 1958, the British Transport Commission announced it had decided to close the line. There was little opposition to the closure and so on October 18th, 1958 the line closed completely.

The Malton & Driffield Junction Railway was authorised by the act of June 26th 1846. Its association with the Malton & Thirsk branch, which was promoted by the York, Newcastle & Berwick Railway offered a through route between the North East and Hull. The sceme was of such strategic importance that George Hudson invested £40,000 of the York & North Midland Railway's money in the Malton & Driffield railway.

Although only 19 miles long The Malton - Driffield line proved costly to build, due to engineering problems. Thousands of tons of stone had to be sunk to provide foundation for the track between Wharram Percy and North Grimston. Hard rock was encounted in the Peafield Cutting and a tunnel had to be built north of Burdale. A number of steep gradients made for difficult working. The railway was built as single track with passing loops at the stations.

Following Hudson's downfall and the economic climate, the York, Newcastle & Berwick became reluctant to build the Thirsk - Malton section and it was only following court action that the through route was built. Both lines opening on May 19th, 1853.

With the formation of the North Eastern Railway in 1854, the Malton & Driffield was incorporated at its own request into the amalgamated company.

As the line passed through a sparsely populated rural area passenger traffic was never heavy. The service, which ran on weekdays only, consisted of 3 stopping trains a day in each direction.

However the railway was a blessing to those who farmed on the Wolds, especially during the winter months when the roads became blocked by snowdrifts.

The main source of freight was stone from the large quarries at Burdale and Wharram which was dispatched to the steelworks on Teesside. In 1925 Wharram traffic alone amounted to 104,808 tons of chalk in 7,885 wagons, whilst normal agricultural freight amounted to 2,447 tons in 424 wagons.

On June 3rd, 1950 British Railways withdrew the normal

A class J27 O-6-O engine No.65844 calls at Settrington station with the afternoon return pick up goods between Malton - Driffield in the 1950's. PHOTOGRAPH NEVILLE STEAD COLLECTION.

Wharram station looking towards Malton. The engine working the pick up goods which ran on Tuesdays and Thursdays is engaged in shunting duties. Scenic excursions travelling over the line stopped at Wharram for water and this gave passengers the chance to get off the train to stretch their legs. PHOTOGRAPH TONY ROSS.

A 1956 view of North Grimston station looking south towards Driffield. Engines heading in this direction faced a stiff climb up the 1 in 73 gradient to Wharram.
PHOTOGRAPH TONY ROSS.

Botanic Gardens shed B1 4-6-O No.61010 "Wildebeeste" attacks the 1 in 71 gradient through the station at Burdale, with a scenic excursion to the Yorkshire Moors and Coast, on Bank Holiday Sunday, August 3rd, 1958. The tour from Hull left at 10.30 am and cost 13/-. Heading north it branched off onto the Driffield - Malton line, then Malton - Pickering - Grosmont to Whitby (1.5 hours stay). It returned home via the coastal line through Robins Hood's Bay to Scarborough (staying 3.75 hours). Then to Hull via Bridlington, arriving back at Paragon station at 8 pm.
PHOTOGRAPH TONY ROSS.

British Railways staff at Sledmere & Fimber on September 25th, 1958. From left to right: porter, station master, guard, fireman and driver. The engine which is working the pick up goods is J39 0-6-0 No. 64928 from Malton shed.
PHOTOGRAPH TONY ROSS.

A pick up goods shunting stock at Sledmere & Fimber station in the 1950's. This small rural station was close to Sledmere House and on several occasions royal trains drawn by top link main line engines arrived with members of the royal household during their visits to the area.
PHOTOGRAPH J.F SEDGWICK.

On January 12th, 1958 due to the rural roads being blocked by snowdrifts. British Railways sent out a special relief train to provide badly needed supplies for stranded villagers and farmers in the vicinity of the Malton - Driffield line. This view shows the train heading in the direction of Driffield on the flat section of track near Wetwang.
PHOTOGRAPH INNES STUDIO - HESSLE.

A 1950's view of Wetwang station. Following the withdrawal of passenger services from the Malton - Driffield line in 1950, the stations remained open for the carriage of goods until full closure in 1958. *PHOTOGRAPH TONY ROSS.*

After the passage of the 10.10 am Malton - Driffield pick up goods train across Garton Slack level crossing which was situated between Wetwang and Garton, the guard re-opens the gates to road traffic. The road is the A166 Stamford Bridge - Fridaythorpe - Driffield. This photograph was taken on September 25th, 1958 a few weeks before the gates were closed for the last time. *PHOTOGRAPH TONY ROSS.*

MALTON TO DRIFFIELD

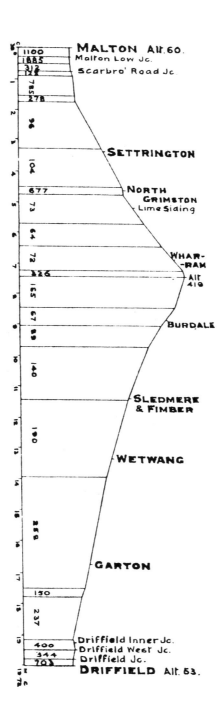

Table 31   MALTON and DRIFFIELD

Week Days only

Miles	Station		a.m		a.m.		p.m		
	29 YORK .... dep		4 30	..	10 15	..	5 17	..	..
	Malton .... dep	Malton to Bridlington	7 0	..	11 0	..	5 58	..	..
3½	Settrington		7 8	..	11 8	..	6 6	..	..
4¾	North Grimston		7 11	..	11 11	..	6 9	..	..
6¾	Wharram		7 16	..	11 16	..	6 14	..	..
9	Burdale		7 21	..	11 21	..	6 19	..	..
11¼	Sledmere and Fimber.		7 26	..	11 26	..	6 24	..	..
13¼	Wetwang		7 30	..	11 30	..	6 28	..	..
16¼	Garton		7 36	..	11 36	..	6 34	..	..
20	Driffield .... arr		7 42	..	11 42	..	6 40	..	..
31½	24 BRIDLINGTON .. arr		8 14	..	1b16	..	7 40	..	..
39½	24 HULL .... ʜ		8 45	..	1c30	..	7 32	..	..

Week Days only

Miles	Station		a.m		a.m		p.m	
	24 HULL .... dep	Bridlington to Malton	7 43	..	1040	..	6 55	..
	24 BRIDLINGTON ..... ʜ		8 30	..	11y0	..	7 0	..
—	Driffield .... dep		8 56	..	12 0	..	7 30	..
3½	Garton		9 3	..	12p7	..	7 37	..
6½	Wetwang		9 9	..	1213	..	7 43	..
8½	Sledmere and Fimber..		9 14	..	1218	..	7 48	..
11	Burdale		9 20	..	1224	..	7 54	..
13½	Wharram		9 25	..	1229	..	7 59	..
15½	North Grimston		9 29	..	1233	..	8 3	..
16½	Settrington		9 32	..	1236	..	8 6	..
20	**Malton** .... arr		9 39	..	1243	..	8 15	..
41½	29 YORK .... arr		11y25	..	1 40	..	9 6	..

b Arr. 12 6 p.m. on Saturdays 25th June to 10th September inclusive.   *c* Arr. 12 45 p.m. on Saturdays   *p* p.m.   **T C** Through Carriages   ɴ Dep. 11 15 a.m. on Saturdays   ʏ Arr. 11 12 a.m. on Mondays and 11 15 a.m. on Saturdays

THE HULL & HOLDERNESS RAILWAY

The Hull & Holderness Railway was promoted by Anthony Banister, a great figure in mid Victorian Hull.

In building this line to the coast of south Holderness there were the financial incentives of linking the industrial port of Hull with the wealthy agricultural area of East Yorkshire. Plus the development of a coastal village into a seaside resort, for the benefit of the people of Hull and West Yorkshire. After a survey of the coast between Easington and Tunstall the village of Withernsea was chosen to be the resort.

The act to build the railway was unopposed and received Royal assent on July 8th, 1853.

The line proved easy to build on the flat terrain of Holderness. It was designed to link as many villages as possible on its route to the coast. The railway was built as single track with passing loops at the stations. The Hull & Holderness Railway was opened on June 26th, 1853. The Hull terminus was the Victoria Dock station which was shared with the York & North Midland until November 1st, 1854.

The Hull & Holderness Railway was one of the truly independent railway companies in that it owned its locomotives and coaches, whereas other small companies relied on larger companies to run their trains.

Despite an initial success the Hull & Holderness was too small to be viable, so from January 1st, 1860 it was leased to the North Eastern Railway, which then bought the line on July 7th, 1862.

In 1864 the Victoria Dock branch was doubled as part of a scheme to allow the Withernsea line trains to run into Hull Paragon, but due to incomplete signalling the move from Victoria Dock station was delayed until June 1st, 1864.

Early in the twentieth century the line was upgraded to double track, except for the sections between Hedon - Ryehill and Ottringham - Winestead. In 1904 the passenger service was withdrawn from Winestead.

In 1948, a halt was opened for speedway enthusiasts on the site of the old Hedon airfield, but it closed after a short spell in use.

The operation of the coastal branches changed very little over the years. Then in the mid 1950's as British Railways looked to diesel power as part of their economy and modernisation plans, a number of new "diesel multiple unit" rail cars were sent to Hull. On Monday January 7th, 1957 the Hull - Withernsea service was chosen for the inaugural run of the new diesel railcar service for the Hull area.

Then from January 4th, 1960 in a cost cutting exercise station staff were withdrawn from the intermediate stations.

The 1963 Beeching report listed the Hull - Withernsea line for closure. Originally British Railways planned to end passenger services on September 9th 1963, but due to objections this date was withdrawn.

On January 6th, 1964 the Transport Users Consultative Committee heard over 80 objections to closure backed by a 15,000 signature petition from holidaymakers.

The main argument against closure was Withernsea's reliance on the large number of daytrippers which were attracted to the resort by the convenience of rail travel (Local pick up points). Some 35,000 passengers per month travelled in peak season, with an annual total of about 132,000.

In addition some 200 local people used the service to commute to work in Hull. Furthermore goods travel on the line was substantial, an estimated 800 tons of coal being carried each month.

On September 14th, 1964 Mr. Marples the Minister of Transport announced the closure of passenger services on the line with effect from October 17th, 1964.

On Thursday October 15th, 1964 the Conservative Government was defeated in the General Election. This led to dramatic last minute attempts to halt the closure of the Withernsea and Hornsea lines. Appeals were telegrammed to Prime Minister Harold Wilson and East Hull M.P. Commander Harry Pursey travelled to London to lobby for the retention of the lines.

The last passenger trains ran on Saturday evening October 17th. They were the 6.25pm to Withernsea and 6.55pm to Hornsea. On the return workings to Hull the train buffers were adorned with wreaths as the communities mourned the loss of their railway service.

Hopes for the re-instatement of passenger services were soon dashed. It transpired that the new Labour Government were as keen to implement branch line closure as the outgoing Conservatives had been.

The through goods service lingered on until April 30th, 1965.

Marfleet was a small suburban station at the eastern edge of the city, close to King George Dock. The station remained open for goods traffic until May 1st, 1972 long after the demise of the passenger service.
PHOTOGRAPH J.F. SEDGWICK.

At Hedon station on July 5th, 1958 the signalman is issuing the driver of a train to Withernsea with the token which allows him to gain access to the section of single line between Hedon and Ryehill & Burstwick. Hedon station was served by one platform which was situated on the south side of the line.
PHOTOGRAPH J.F.SEDGWICK.

During summer months the popular resort of Withernsea attracted a large amount of "day tripper" excursion traffic. Occasionally these were worked through to the coast by main line engines. Stanier class Black Five 4-6-O No.45238 approaches Hedon with a return excursion train from Withernsea - Chesterfield Midland.
PHOTOGRAPH D. LECKONBY.

The driver of a train to Withernsea surrenders the single line token to the signalman at Ryehill & Burstwick and passes on to call at the station. On summer weekends the eight car sets were filled to capacity as the people of Hull headed to the "beach".
PHOTOGRAPH NEVILLE STEAD COLLECTION.

Keyingham station looking east towards Withernsea. This station was in the double track section between Ryehill & Burstwick - Ottringham.
PHOTOGRAPH J.F. SEDGWICK.

Patrington station looking east to Withernsea on October 5th, 1964 shortly before the withdrawal of the passenger services on the line. The station which served one of the larger communities in the Holderness area was of a similar design to the others on the line.
PHOTOGRAPH J.F. SEDGWICK.

A train load of workers and shoppers arrive at Withernsea station on a bleak rainy day, part of the 200 or so local people who used the line to commute to Hull. In the background is the former Station Hotel, which was purchased by Sir James & Francis Reckitt in 1902 and presented to the Hull Royal Infirmary as a convalescent home.
PHOTOGRAPH AUTHOR'S COLLECTION.

HULL AND WITHERNSEA
23rd MAY to 25th SEPTEMBER 1949

Table 22

WEEKDAYS

	am	am	am	B am	am	am	SO am	SO pm	SX pm	SO pm	pm	pm	pm	pm	SO pm	pm
York .... dep	3 40	...	...	...	8 20	10 10	10 45	10 45	12 15	12 25	3 25	...	5 5	5 22	7 15	...
Leeds (City) .... „	3c14	...	...	7 3	8 25	9 45	11 45	11 50	12 20	1 35	3 25	...	5 7	6 38	...	...
HULL .... dep	5 50	6 35	7 33	9 30	10 15	12 11	12 40	1 9	1 30	2 0	4 35	5 27	5 40	6 25	7 45	9 20
Botanic Gardens .... „	...	6 39	7 37	9 34	10 19	12 15	12 44	1 13	1 34	2 4	4 39	...	5 44	6 29	7 49	9 24
Stepney .... „	...	...	7 40	9 37	10 22	12 18	12 47	1 16	1 37	2 7	4 42	...	5 47	6 32	7 52	9 27
Wilmington .... „	...	6 43	7 43	9 40	10 25	12 21	12 50	1 19	1 40	2 10	4 45	5 32	5 50	6 35	7 55	9 30
Southcoates .... „	...	...	7 46	9 43	10 28	12 24	12 53	1 22	1 43	2 13	4 48	5 35	5 53	6 38	7 58	9 33
Marfleet .... „	...	...	7 51	9 48	10 33	12 29	12 58	1 27	1 48	2 18	4 53	...	5 58	6 43	8 3	9 38
Hedon .... „	6 6	...	7 57	...	10 39	12 35	1 4	1 33	1 54	2 24	4 59	...	6 4	6 49	8 9	9 44
Rye Hill and Burstwick „	...	6 59	8 3	...	10 45	12 41	1 10	1 39	2 0	2 30	5 5	...	6 10	6 55	8 15	9 50
Keyingham .... „	...	7 3	8 7	...	10 49	12 45	...	1 43	2 4	2 34	5 9	...	6 14	6 59	8 19	9 54
Ottringham .... „	6 18	7 7	8 11	...	10 53	12 49	...	1 47	2 8	2 38	5 13	...	6 18	7 3	8 23	9 58
Patrington .... „	6 24	7 13	8 17	...	10 59	12 55	1 21	1 53	2 14	2 44	5 19	...	6 24	7 9	8 29	10 4
WITHERNSEA .... arr	6 31	7 20	8 24	10 12	11 6	1 2	1 28	2 0	2 21	2 51	5 26	6 3	6 31	7 16	8 36	10 11

WEEKDAYS

	am	am	am	am	am	pm	SO pm	SO pm	pm	pm	pm	B pm	pm	SO pm	pm	pm
WITHERNSEA .... dep	6 43	7 47	8 18	8 43	11 40	1 50	2 18	2 50	4 24	5 57	6 25	6 45	7 30	8 35	9 0	10 30
Patrington .... „	6 50	7 54	...	8 52	11 47	1 57	2 25	2 57	4 31	6 4	6 32	6 52	7 37	8 42	9 7	10 37
Ottringham .... „	6 56	8 0	...	8 58	11 53	2 3	2 31	3 3	4 37	6 10	6 38	6 58	7 43	8 48	9 13	10 43
Keyingham .... „	7 0	8 4	...	9 2	11 57	2 7	2 35	3 7	4 41	6 14	6 42	7 2	7 47	8 52	9 17	10 47
Rye Hill and Burstwick „	7 4	8 8	...	9 6	12 1	2 11	2 39	3 11	4 45	6 18	6 46	7 6	7 51	8 56	9 21	10 51
Hedon .... „	7 10	8 14	...	9 12	12 7	2 17	2 45	3 17	4 51	6 24	6 52	7 12	7 57	9 2	9 27	10 57
Marfleet .... „	7 16	8 20	...	...	12 13	2 23	2 51	3 23	4 57	6 32	6 58	7 18	8 3	9 8	9 33	11 3
Southcoates .... „	7 21	8 25	8 46	9 21	12 18	2 28	2 56	3 28	5 2	6 35	7 3	7 23	8 8	9 13	9 38	11 8
Wilmington .... „	7 24	8 28	8 49	...	12 21	2 31	2 59	3 31	5 5	6 38	7 6	7 26	8 11	9 16	9 41	11 11
Stepney .... „	7 27	8 31	...	...	12 24	2 34	3 2	3 34	5 8	6 41	7 9	7 29	8 14	9 19	9 44	11 14
Botanic Gardens .... „	7 30	8 34	...	...	12 27	2 37	3 5	3 37	5 11	6 44	7 12	7 32	8 17	9 22	9 47	11 17
HULL .... arr	7 34	8 39	8 54	9 29	12 31	2 41	3 9	3 41	5 15	6 48	7 16	7 36	8 21	9 26	9 51	11 21
Leeds (City) .... arr	9 35	10 9	...	...	12 11	2 14	4 45	...	5 10	...	8 36	...	10 11	...	...	...
York .... „	8 58	...	...	...	11 10	4 1	...	...	5 31	...	8 40	9 11	12b32	...	...	...

SUNDAYS

	am	C am	C am	pm	pm
York .... dep	...	...	...	9a30	4 20
Leeds (City) .... „	3 25	...	...	...	4 45
HULL .... dep	8 5	9 10	9 40	1 5	7 5
Botanic Gardens .... „	8 9	9 14	9 44	1 9	7 9
Stepney .... „	8 12	9 17	9 47	1 12	7 12
Wilmington .... „	8 15	9 20	9 50	1 15	7 15
Southcoates .... „	8 18	9 24	9 53	1 18	7 18
Marfleet .... „	8 23	...	9 58	1 23	7 23
Hedon .... „	8 29	...	10 4	1 29	7 29
Rye Hill and Burstwick „	8 35	...	10 10	1 35	7 35
Keyingham .... „	8 39	...	10 14	1 39	7 39
Ottringham .... „	8 43	...	10 18	1 43	7 43
Patrington .... „	8 49	...	10 24	1 49	7 49
WITHERNSEA .... arr	8 56	9 55	10 31	1 56	7 56

SUNDAYS

	am	C pm	C pm	pm	pm
WITHERNSEA .... dep	9 20	5 15	6 20	7 20	8 20
Patrington .... „	9 27	...	...	...	8 27
Ottringham .... „	9 33	...	...	...	8 33
Keyingham .... „	9 37	...	...	...	8 37
Rye Hill and Burstwick „	9 41	...	...	...	8 41
Hedon .... „	9 47	...	6 43	...	8 47
Marfleet .... „	9 53	...	6 49	7 50	8 53
Southcoates .... „	9 58	5 46	6 54	7 55	8 58
Wilmington .... „	10 1	5 50	6 58	7 59	9 1
Stepney .... „	10 4	5 53	7 1	8 3	9 4
Botanic Gardens .... „	10 7	5 56	7 4	8 7	9 7
HULL .... arr	10 11	6 0	7 8	8 11	9 11
Leeds (City) .... arr	3 p0	...	...	...	8 48
York .... „	5 25	...	...	7 55	10 9

A—For other trains between Hull and Wilmington see Sheet NE 10. B—Saturdays only. Not after 10th September
C—Not after 11th September. SO—Saturdays only SX—Saturdays excepted
a—am b—Sundays mornings excepted. p—pm c—On Mondays leaves Leeds 3-20 am

HULL & HORNSEA RAILWAY

Originally a branch line to link Hornsea to the Hull - Bridlington line at Arram was sanctioned in 1846. But due to the financial position of the York & North Midland following the downfall of George Hudson the project was postponed.

The Hull & Hornsea Railway was promoted by Joseph Armytage Wade, a Hornsea resident and Hull timber merchant. Mr Wade and his associates were convinced that the "superior residential amenities" which Hornsea had to offer could be developed into a fashionable Victorian watering place.

The Hull & Hornsea Railway Company was formed in 1861 and the act to build the line was passed on June 30th, 1862.

Although the railway ran through reasonably flat terrain, there were many problems in building the line. When it came to making embankments it was found that the local clay soil was unsuitable and ballast from Kelsey Hill had to be brought in. At first it was planned to terminate at Hornsea Bridge station. However it was decided to extend the line down to the sea front. This proved costly due to the land in the area being boggy.

On top of this, certain engineering aspects were not up to standard and had to be rectified. Eventually the government inspector was satisfied and the line opened on March 28th, 1864. The Hull terminus was at the first Wilmington station. The trains were operated by the North Eastern Railway.

The problems with the building of the line caused the company serious financial loss. Construction of the railway had cost about 75% more than anticipated. As receipts from passenger and goods traffic were below expectations the company was soon in financial difficulties. There were many stormy shareholders meetings. The outcome was that a marger with the North Eastern Railway was sought.

This led to the Hull & Hornsea being merged into the North Eastern Railway on July 16th, 1866.

The Line was upgraded to double track early in the twentieth century. To avoid confusion with other stations Goxhill was renamed Wassand in 1904 and Burton Constable renamed Ellerby in 1922. The original Ellerby which was closed in 1902 became known as Ellerby West Siding. Wassand was one of the last market day only stations in the North East. From opening in 1865 to closure in 1953 the station was open for only one day a week and served by one train in each direction.

Following their takeover both the Hornsea and the Withernsea lines were closely associated. In 1957 diesel rail cars were introduced to replace steam trains. To help reduce operating costs, from January 4th, 1960 station staff were withdrawn from all the intermediate stations. The function of issuing tickets to passengers joining at these stations became the duty of the train guard.

However the two coastal branches still required a large complement of operating staff to work the many level crossings and their attendant signal boxes.

The Centralised Traffic Control scheme which was to have been pioneered on the York - Beverley line was to be extended to cover the Hornsea line starting at Wilmington and the Withernsea branch starting from Hedon. From these locations the line was to be singled, level crossings were to be automated and traffic on the lines controlled from Hull.

Unfortnately the CTC scheme was abandoned. British Railways in a change of direction began looking to justify closing unprofitable lines and the high cost of traditional operation worked in their favour.

The Hornsea branch was listed for closure in the 1963 Beeching Report and like Withernsea the local authorities campaigned against closure, supported by a 3,000 signature petition.

Traffic figures for 1962, for Hornsea's two stations were approximately 60,000 tickets issued and 120,000 collected mainly from daytrippers. In addition there were many local passholders among the 340 local residents who used the service on a daily basis. Also apart from the usual coal freight traffic, in the first 3 months of 1963 some 3,000 chests of goods were carried from the local pottery.

On September 14th, 1964 the Minister of Transport gave British Railways consent to withdraw passenger services from the line, despite the Transport Users Consultative Committee advising that closure would lead to hardship for the local communities. The last passenger trains ran on October 17th.

Goods traffic was withdrawn from April 30th, 1965 and the track was lifted.

Bound for Hornsea, a class A8 4-6-2 tank engine No.69855 passes into the suburbs north of Stoneferry crossing on Chamberlain Road, towards Sutton on Hull station.
PHOTOGRAPH AUTHOR'S COLLECTION.

The railway at Sutton was well placed to serve the local community being close to the centre of the village. The station platforms with the two waiting rooms were situated in a cutting. The main station offices and booking hall were up at street level. This view looking towards Hull was taken on October 10th, 1964.
PHOTOGRAPH IAN SCOTNEY.

Class L1 2-6-4 tank engine No. 67766 passes through Swine station with a Hornsea to Hull extra in July 1955. The station was situated a good way from the small rural community it served.
PHOTOGRAPH JOHN OXLEY.

A stopping train for Hornsea calls at Ellerby station circa 1960. Like Sutton on Hull the platform buildings were sparse, with the main building at street level. Ellerby was renamed from Burton Constable in 1922.
PHOTOGRAPH NEVILLE STEAD COLLECTION.

A view of Sigglesthorpe station, from the down platform looking towards Hornsea. The station was of a similar design to Swine, having a staggered down platform dating from when the railway was converted to double track. The North Eastern Railway used this option rather than re-siting the goods yard and coal cells.
PHOTOGRAPH J.F. SEDGWICK.

Hornsea Bridge station looking east towards the sea. Originally to have been the terminus, the station was situated on an embankment near to the outskirts of the town. The station had a large goods yard which dealt with most of the town's goods traffic. Being at ground level it was reached by a spur located on level land to the west of the station.
PHOTOGRAPH DOUGLAS THOMPSON.

At Hornsea Town station the footplate crew of Class C12 4-4-2 tank locomotive No.67371 have a chat with holiday makers whilst waiting departure time on a service train for Hull. The island platform on the left was used for excursion trains. Being just a short train ride from Hull the resort was very popular with daytrippers and on Summer Sundays an average of some 6,000 people would pass through this station en route to the beach which was just a short distance away.
PHOTOGRAPH A.J. WICKENS.

HULL TO WITHERNSEA

HULL TO HORNSEA

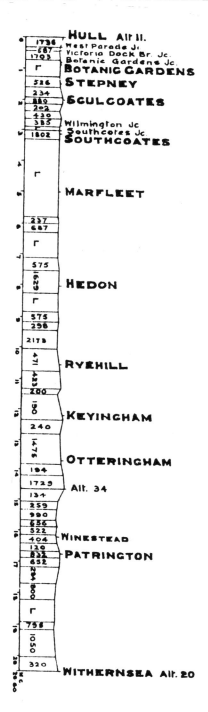

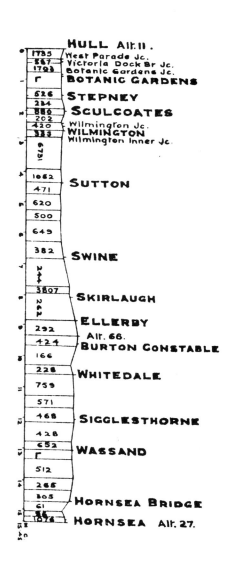

HULL AND HORNSEA
23rd MAY to 25th SEPTEMBER 1949

Table 21

WEEKDAYS

		am	am	am	am	am	pm	SO	D am	pm	pm	pm	pm	SO pm	pm		
York	dep	3 40	...	...	8 20	10 10	...		10 45	12 25	3 25	...	5 5	5 22	7 15	...	...
Leeds (City)	„	3c14	...	...	8 25	9 45	...		11d50	1 35	3 25	...	5 7	6 38	...	...	...
						noon			pm								
HULL	dep	6 0	6 45	7 40	10 0	12 0	12 45		1 40	4 20	5 18	5 50	6 30	7 55	9 25	...	...
Botanic Gardens	„	...	6 49	7 44	10 4	12 4	12 49		1 44	4 24	...	5 54	6 34	7 59	9 29	...	...
Stepney	„	...	6 52	7 47	10 7	12 7	12 52		1 47	4 27	...	5 57	6 37	8 2	9 32	...	...
Wilmington	„	...	...	7 50	10 10	12 10	12 55		1 50	4 30	5 23	6 0	6 40	8 5	9 35	...	...
Sutton-on-Hull	„	6 9	...	7 55	10 15	12 15	1 0		1 55	4 35	5 28	6 5	6 45	8 10	9 40	...	...
Swine	„	6 14	...	8 0	...	12 20	...		2 0	4 40	...	6 10	6 50	8 15	9 45	...	...
Skirlaugh	„	6 18	...	8 4	...	...	...		2 4	4 44	...	6 14	6 54	8 19	9 49	...	...
Ellerby	„	...	7 5	8 8	10 24	12 26	1 9		2 8	4 48	5 37	6 18	6 58	8 23	9 53	...	...
Whitedale	„	...	7 8	8 11	...	12 29	...		2 11	4 51	...	6 21	7 1	8 26	9 56	...	...
Sigglesthorne	„	6 25	...	8 15	...	12 33	...		2 15	4 55	...	6 25	7 5	8 30	10 0	...	...
Hornsea Bridge	„	6 30	7 15	8 20	10 33	12 38	1 18		2 20	5 0	5 46	6 30	7 10	8 35	10 5	...	...
HORNSEA	arr	6 32	7 17	8 22	10 35	12 40	1 20		2 22	5 2	5 48	6 32	7 12	8 37	10 7	...	...

WEEKDAYS

		am	am	am	am	C am	pm	SO pm	pm	pm	pm	pm	pm	SO pm	pm		
HORNSEA	dep	7 14	7 50	8 28	8 50	10 55	1 4	1 50	2 50	5 30	6 25	7 25	8 40	9 0	10 30	...	...
Hornsea Bridge	„	7 17	7 53	8 31	8 53	10 58	1 7	1 53	2 53	5 33	6 28	7 28	8 43	9 3	10 33	...	...
Sigglesthorne	„	...	7 58	8 36	8 58	11 3	1 12	1 58	2 58	5 38	6 33	7 33	8 48	9 8	10 38	...	...
Whitedale	„	...	8 2	...	...	11 7	1 16	2 2	3 2	5 42	...	7 37	8 52	9 12	10 42	...	...
Ellerby	„	7 26	8 5	8 41	9 3	11 10	1 19	2 5	3 5	5 45	6 38	7 40	8 55	9 15	10 45	...	...
Skirlaugh	„	...	8 9	...	...	11 14	1 23	2 9	3 9	5 49	6 42	...	...	9 19	10 49	...	...
Swine	„	...	8 13	...	...	11 18	1 27	2 13	3 13	5 53	...	7 46	9 1	9 23	10 53	...	...
Sutton-on-Hull	„	7 35	8 18	8 50	9 12	11 23	1 32	2 18	3 18	5 58	6 49	7 51	9 6	9 28	10 58	...	...
Wilmington	„	7 40	8 23	8 55	9 17	11 28	1 37	2 23	3 23	6 3	6 54	7 55	9 11	9 33	11 3	...	...
Stepney	„	7 43	8 26	8 58	...	11 31	1 40	2 26	3 26	6 6	6 57	7 59	9 14	9 36	11 6	...	...
Botanic Gardens	„	7 46	8 29	9 1	...	11 34	1 43	2 29	3 29	6 9	7 0	8 2	9 17	9 39	11 9	...	...
HULL	arr	7 50	8 33	9 5	9 22	11 38	1 47	2 33	3 33	6 13	7 4	8 6	9 21	9 43	11 13	...	...
Leeds (City)	arr	9S43	10 9	...	12 11	2F14	3 12	4 45	5 10	...	8 36	10 11	...	...	...	...	...
York	„	8 58	...	...	11 10	1p31	4 1	4 1	5 31	...	8 40	12b32	...	...	...	...	...

SUNDAYS

		am	am	B pm	pm	
York	dep	...	...	9a42	4 20	...
Leeds (City)	„	3 25	...	9 30	4 45	...
HULL	dep	8 15	9 20	1 15	7 10	...
Botanic Gardens	„	8 19	9 24	1 19	7 14	...
Stepney	„	8 22	9 27	1 22	7 17	...
Wilmington	„	8 25	9 30	1 25	7 20	...
Sutton-on-Hull	„	8 30	9 35	1 30	7 25	...
Swine	„	8 35	...	1 35	7 30	...
Skirlaugh	„	...	...	1 39	7 34	...
Ellerby	„	8 41	...	1 43	7 38	...
Whitedale	„	8 44	...	1 46	7 41	...
Sigglesthorne	„	8 48	...	1 50	7 45	...
Hornsea Bridge	„	8 53	...	1 55	7 50	...
HORNSEA	arr	8 55	9 55	1 57	7 52	...

SUNDAYS

		am	B pm	pm	pm	
HORNSEA	dep	9 20	6 30	7 0	8 15	...
Hornsea Bridge	„	9 23	6 33	...	8 18	...
Sigglesthorne	„	9 28	6 38	...	8 23	...
Whitedale	„	9 32	6 42	...	8 27	...
Ellerby	„	9 35	6 45	...	8 30	...
Skirlaugh	„	...	6 49	...	8 34	...
Swine	„	9 41	6 53	...	8 38	...
Sutton-on-Hull	„	9 46	6 58	7 22	8 43	...
Wilmington	„	9 51	7 3	7 27	8 48	...
Stepney	„	9 54	7 6	7 31	8 51	...
Botanic Gardens	„	9 57	7 9	7 34	8 54	...
HULL	arr	10 1	7 13	7 38	8 58	...
Leeds (City)	arr	3 p0	10 11	10 11	...	...
York	„	5p25	10 9	10 9	...	...

A—For other trains between Hull and Wilmington see Sheet NE 11. **B**—Not after 11th September **C**—On Mondays calls at Wassand (between Sigglesthorne and Hornsea Bridge) to take up for Hull **D**—on Mondays calls at Wassand (between Sigglesthorne and Hornsea Bridge) to set down from Hull. **F**—On Saturdays arrives Leeds 1-43 pm **S or SO**—Saturdays only **a**—am **b**—Sunday mornings excepted **c**—On Mondays leaves Leeds 3-20 am **d**—On Saturdays leaves Leeds 11-45 am **p**—pm

THE HULL & BARNSLEY RAILWAY

Various schemes for lines from Hull to the West Riding had been proposed over the years. As early as 1845 a Hull & Barnsley Junction Railway had been proposed and suppressed.

By the 1870's the Hull docks were struggling to cope with the upsurge in trade and in an attempt to ease the situation the North Eastern Railway began to divert traffic to Hartlepool, Goole and Grimsby. This outraged local business concerns and there were calls for a railway system independent of the North Eastern Railway.

The Hull, Barnsley and West Riding Junction Railway and Dock Company was formed on May 28th, 1879 following a meeting of an influential group of merchants, bankers and shipowners at the Royal Station Hotel, Hull. To most of the sponsors the more important part of the scheme was to be the building of a new deep water dock constructed to the east of the existing ones.

The following year the plans for the new railway were laid before Parliament. The Hull Corporation agreed to sell to the Railway Company 126 acres of land on the site of what was to become the Alexandra Dock. Although the North Eastern Railway and the Hull Dock Company opposed the HB & WRJR & DCO'S petition, the act received Royal assent on August 26th, 1880.

On January 15th, 1881 a ceremony to mark the cutting of the first sod of earth by Chairman, Gerard Smith, was held on the site of the Company's new dock. During construction of the railway costs escalated far beyond the original estimates. Great engineering difficulties were encountered due to the nature of Hull's subsoil and the hard chalk encountered in cuttings and tunnels on the Wolds' section of the route. Also the purchase of land and station buildings cost more than expected. By 1884, as a result of the Company's inability to pay the contractors, work was suspended. Later in the year work was resumed after a further injection of capital was raised from an issue of shares.

In the face of enormous difficulties, both engineering and financial, the Hull & Barnsley project was finally completed in 1885 at a cost of almost £6 million, becoming one of the last major independent railway projects completed in this country. The Company's Alexandra Dock was opened on July 16th. Freight traffic commenced 4 days later and on July 27th passengers were carried for the first time. The passenger terminus was at Cannon Street, some half mile short of the proposed terminus nearer to the city centre at Charlotte Street.

Initial traffic did not reach the expected high level and within a very short time the Company was in financial difficulties. An amalgamation with the Midland Railway or the North Eastern was proposed but due to strenuous opposition all such schemes proved abortive.

Gradually the Hull & Barnsley's fortunes began to improve and a degree of prosperity was enjoyed. Coal shipments grew. In 1880 the port of Hull had handled 600,000 tons, by 1900 it increased to 2,200,000 tons the bulk of which was loaded at Alexandra Dock. To cope with the increase in coal export shipments the dock was extended in 1899. For the return workings the coal wagons were loaded with imported pit props for use in the mines. Another important commodity the railway carried was Australian and New Zealand wool, for use in the West Yorkshire clothing industry.

From July 1st, 1905 the Company's title was shortened to the Hull & Barnsley Railway Company Ltd.

Powers granted to the North Eastern and Hull & Barnsley Railway Companies enabled them to undertake the construction of a jointly owned deepwater dock on land to the east of Alexandra Dock. Work commenced in 1906 and was completed in 1914. The cost of construction was mainly borne by the N.E.R. The new dock was named after His Majesty King George V who performed the opening ceremony on June 26th, 1914.

As a prelude to the grouping of 1923, the Hull & Barnsley was amalgamated with the North Eastern on April 1st, 1922, just nine months before the formation of the London & North Eastern Railway Company.

In 1924 a spur was installed at Spring Bank connecting the former H & B and N.E.R. lines. This was done as an economy measure: it allowed H & B passenger trains to run into Paragon Station from July 13th, 1924 and permitted the closure of the Beverley Road and Cannon Street stations although the latter was used for goods traffic until 1964.

On the April 8th, 1929 the Springhead Halt was opened for passengers.

In LNER days, the export coal traffic to Hull from the South Yorkshire collieries continued to be brisk, but through passenger traffic between Hull and Cudworth was sparse and so from January 1st, 1932 the LNER ordered the withdrawal of passenger services West of South Howden.

During the 1950's British Railways began to close loss-making branch lines and in 1955 they turned their attention to the Hull - South Howden service. Despite opposition from the local authorities the passenger service was withdrawn from July 30th, 1955. Excursion trains continued to run until 1958.

At one time British Railways planned to build a spur at Eastrington between the H & B and the NER Leeds lines in order to eliminate the expensive operating section through the Wolds, but this scheme was dropped (mainly due to declining coal exports) and from November 1958 all through traffic was diverted away from the H & B. A pick up freight to Carlton ran until April 1959 when the whole line between Little Weighton and Wrangbrook Junction was closed completely. As of July 4th, 1964 the pick up freight to Little Weighton ceased.

At the present time the former H & B high level line between King George Dock and Hessle Road Junction is still in use for rail freight movement from the dock and Saltend refinery.

Springhead Halt was opened by the London & North Eastern Railway on April 8th, 1929. Arriving at the halt with the 12.20 pm Hull - North Cave service is class G5 0-4-4 tank engine No.67282. Normally on push and pull workings the engine would be running bunker first, but as the train is conveying a horse box the engine is facing "right way".
PHOTOGRAPH JOHN OXLEY.

A 1950's view of Willerby and Kirkella station facing in the direction of Hull. The station was situated on an embankment which carried the line through the adjoining villages of Willerby and Kirkella. At ground level were the ticket and parcels offices, also the booking hall. On the first floor leading to the platforms were the waiting rooms and porters' room. The station master's quarters accounted for a substantial part of the main station building. Class WD 2-8-O No.90571 is shunting the yard on a pick up goods.
PHOTOGRAPH NEVILLE STEAD.

Near Skidby, a Stanier class 8F 2-8-O No.48670 is hard at work with a train of empty coal wagons on the 1 in 100 climb towards the summit of the line at Little Weighton.
PHOTOGRAPH LANCE BROWN (NEVILLE STEAD COLLECTION).

On push and pull workings when the engine was at the rear of the train the driver controlled the train from a compartment in the front coach, whilst the fireman was left in charge of the engine. As seen in this view of a push and pull train at the west end of Sugar Loaf tunnel.
PHOTOGRAPH JOHN OXLEY.

Little Weighton station viewed through the road bridge facing west towards Drewton tunnel. It was a shame that a railway with such fine station buildings did not attract the volume of passengers it deserved.
PHOTOGRAPH AUTHOR'S COLLECTION.

A class B1 4-6-O No.61256 with a goods train, coasts down the incline through the cutting at the west end of Drewton tunnel towards South Cave in May 1959, shortly after the official closure of this section of the line.
PHOTOGRAPH NEVILLE STEAD.

As WD class engine No.90322 storms up the incline with a coal train for Hull through South Cave in 1957, time was running out for the Hull and Barnsley. Although the station looks derelict shorn of its fittings the staff are still keeping it tidy. South Cave station was of the same design as South Howden.
PHOTOGRAPH TONY ROSS.

WD class engine No.90571 was regularly roistered for the pick up goods working from Neptune street to Carlton Towers. As it passes through North Cave workmen are stripping the station of its canopies and waiting shelter, following the withdrawal of passenger services in 1955. North Cave which was identical in size and shape to Willerby and Kirkella was one of the stations fitted with wooden platforms.
PHOTOGRAPH NEVILLE STEAD.

At Wallingfen the line ran on an embankment. The station buildings were situated at ground level on the north side of the line. The train arriving on the down platform in this 1955 view, is the 5.47 pm South Howden - Hull worked by G5 O-4-4 tank engine No.67337. Wallingfen was renamed from Newport by the L.N.E.R. in 1923.
PHOTOGRAPH JOHN OXLEY.

The pick up goods calls at Sandholme on its way west to Carlton Towers. The station buildings at Sandholme were located on the south side of the line. Situated on the level section before the climb to the east, Sandholme had extensive sidings where coal trains could be re-sorted into manageable loads for working "over the top" to Hull.
PHOTOGRAPH NEVILLE STEAD.

The small rural community of Eastrington was served by two railway stations, the Hull & Barnsley's "North" Eastrington and the North Eastern Railway's "South" Eastrington. Both stations adopted their prefix when taken over by the L.N.E.R. in 1923. In this sad view taken on May, 1st 1959 some weeks after "official closure" a goods train has delivered a consignment of timber. The once well kept station is almost derelict. The sidings were used to store timber which was delivered from the Hull docks by the pick up goods.
PHOTOGRAPH NEVILLE STEAD.

A view of South Howden facing west, with a push and pull train waiting to depart for Hull. Howden was a town which was served by the two rival railway companies. The Hull & Barnsley's "South" Howden station occupied the prime site near to the centre of the town. The station was the reversal point for passenger services to Hull, following the withdrawal of the through service to Cudworth in 1932.
PHOTOGRAPH JOHN OXLEY.

The remote Barmby station as seen from the rear of a guards van on a freight train which has passed through on its way to Carlton Towers. The station was situated a short distance from the Ouse swing bridge.
PHOTOGRAPH NEVILLE STEAD.

The noise of the engine's exhaust beat and rattling of coal wagons breaks the early morning silence of rural East Yorkshire, as WD No.90396 passes Asselby signal box with a train for Hull.
PHOTOGRAPH J.F. SEDGWICK.

Drax station was yet another fine example of Hull & Barnsley architecture. A WD class freight engine is busy shunting the yard on a pick up goods.
PHOTOGRAPH NEVILLE STEAD.

Carlton Towers station looking west towards Cudworth. The pick up goods train in the siding is shunting stock in preparation for the return working to Hull.
PHOTOGRAPH NEVILLE STEAD.

HULL TO CARLTON

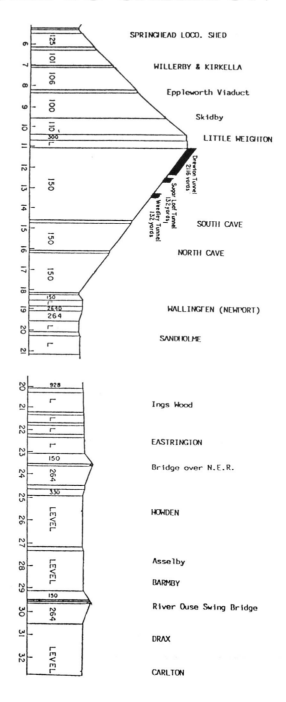

SPRINGHEAD LOCO. SHED

WILLERBY & KIRKELLA

Eppleworth Viaduct

Skidby

LITTLE WEIGHTON

Drewton Tunnel 2116 yards

Sugar Loaf Tunnel 132 yards

Weedley Tunnel 132 yards

SOUTH CAVE

NORTH CAVE

WALLINGFEN (NEWPORT)

SANDHOLME

Ings Wood

EASTRINGTON

Bridge over N.E.R.

HOWDEN

Asselby

BARMBY

River Ouse Swing Bridge

DRAX

CARLTON

126

Table 20 — HULL AND SOUTH HOWDEN

WEEKDAYS

Miles			am	SO am	SX am	SO am	pm	pm	pm	SO pm								
	19 York	dep	3 40	10 10	10 10	10 10	3 10	....	....	6A28	....	....	....	....	....	....	....	....
—	HULL	dep	6 20	11 45	12 20pm	1 15pm	4 30	5 18	5 55	8 30	..	..	..	..	..	..	..	..
3½	Springhead Halt	,,	....	11 54	12 29	1 24	4 39	5 27	6 4	8 39	..	..	..	..	..	..	..	..
4½	Willerby and Kirk Ella ..	,,	6 33	11 59	12 34	1 29	4 44	5 32	6 9	8 44	..	..	..	..	..	..	..	..
8	Little Weighton	,,	6 43	12 9	12 44	1 39	4 54	5 42	6 19	8 54	..	..	..	..	..	..	..	..
12½	South Cave	,,	6 51	12 17	12 52	1 47	5 2	5 50	6 27	9 2	..	..	..	..	..	..	..	..
13½	North Cave	,,	6 55	12 21	12 56	1 51	5 6	5 54	6 31	9 6	..	..	..	..	..	..	..	..
16½	Wallingfen	,,	7 1	12 27	—	1 57	5 12	6 0	6 37	9 12	..	..	..	..	..	..	..	..
17½	Sandholme	,,	7 5	12 31	....	2 1	5 16	6 4	6 41	9 16	..	..	..	..	..	..	..	..
20	North Eastrington Halt ..	,,	..	..	..	..	5 21	..	6 46	9 21	..	..	..	..	..	..	..	..
23	SOUTH HOWDEN ..	arr	7 15	12 41	....	2 11	5 27	6 14	6 52	9 27	..	..	..	..	..	..	..	..

WEEKDAYS

Miles			am	am	am	SO am	SX pm	SO pm	SO pm	pm	pm	SO pm							
—	SOUTH HOWDEN ..	dep	6 40	....	7 53	10 50	....	1 0	2 30	5 47	7 17	10 0	....	....	....	....	..	..	..
3	North Eastrington Halt..	,,	6 46	..	7 59	..	....	1 6	..	..	..	..	..	..	..	..	..	..	..
5½	Sandholme	,,	6 51	....	8 4	11 0	....	1 11	2 40	5 57	7 27	10 10	..	..	..	..	..	..	..
6¼	Wallingfen	,,	6 55	..	8 8	11 4	..	1 15	2 44	6 1	7 31	10 14	..	..	..	..	..	..	..
9½	North Cave............	,,	7 2	..	8 15	11 11	1 6	1 22	2 51	6 8	7 38	10 21	..	..	..	..	..	..	..
10¾	South Cave	,,	7 7	..	8 20	11 16	1 11	1 27	2 56	6 13	7 43	10 26	..	..	..	..	..	..	..
15	Little Weighton	,,	7 17	7 50	8 30	11 26	1 21	1 37	3 6	6 23	7 53	10 36	..	..	..	..	..	..	..
18¼	Willerby and Kirk Ella ..	,,	7 25	7 58	8 38	11 34	1 29	1 45	3 14	6 31	8 1	10 44	..	..	..	..	..	..	..
19¾	Springhead Halt	,,	....	8 2	8 42	11 38	1 33	1 49	....	6 35	8 5	..	..	..	..	..	..	..	..
23	HULL	arr	7 38	8 10	8 50	11 46	1 41	1 57	3 24	6 43	8 13	10 57	..	..	..	..	..	..	..
65½	19 York	arr	8 54	....	11 5	1p31	4 0	4 0	5A19	8A47	12B32	....	....	....	....	....	..	..	..

A—Connection at Selby.
B—am Sunday mornings excepted. Connection at Selby.

SO—Saturdays only.

SX—Saturdays excepted. p—pm.

TIME	DESTINATION	CODE	TIME	DESTINATION	CODE
00.35	MEXBOROUGH	907	13.25	GOOLE	2279
00.55	ICKLES	935	19.00	DRINGHOUSES	2201
01.50	GOOLE	905	19.35	GOOLE	2291
02.05	GOOLE	2207	19.50	ICKLES	915
02.20	CROFT JNC.	2106	20.00	NIDDRIE	332
02.40	YORK	2108	20.40	WHITEMOOR	525
03.25	MILFORD	2179	20.55	MOTTRAM	921
04.15	NEVILLE HILL	2297	21.10	WAKEFIELD	2295
04.20	COLWICK	563	21.45	EAST GOODS	591
06.25	CREWE	909	21.55	ANNERSLEY	917
07.10	COLWICK	537	22.05	BURTON	595
08.35	DONCASTER	557	22.15	NEVILLE HILL	2263
09.40	YORK	2104	22.40	MOTTRAM	921
09.55	WHITEMOOR	527	22.50	SHEFFIELD	901
11.10	SKELTON N.S.	2110	23.00	DONCASTER	593
			23.15	BRADFORD	775
			23.15	SKELTON N.S.	2104

FISH

TIME	DESTINATION	CODE
12.50	BANBURY	601
13.15	NEVILLE HILL	2209
15.32	EAST GOODS	581
18.20	MANCHESTER	2239
18.45	BANBURY	587
18.55	KINGS CROSS	589
19.42	GUIDE BRIDGE	585
20.50	NORMANTON	2249